STATE INTERVENTION IN BRITISH INDUSTRY
1964–68

FRANK BROADWAY

State Intervention in British Industry 1964–68

KAYE & WARD . LONDON

First published by
Kaye & Ward Ltd
194–200 Bishopsgate, London EC2
1969

Copyright © 1969   Frank Broadway
SBN 7182 0799 8

Printed in England by
Adlard & Son Ltd
Dorking, Surrey

Contents

CHAPTER ONE

A rising tide of intervention

When the capitalist world gets into trouble, it always reaches for socialist, interventionist measures, the late Harold Laski used to claim. A good deal of support for this hypothesis can be found in the events of the nineteen-sixties.

In most of the world's advanced industrial nations, governments reacted to the characteristic problems of the decade—inflation, balance of payments deficits, and flagging economic growth rates— by increasing measures of intervention in industry, trade and finance.

France added new elements to an already dirigiste system, including comprehensive price controls on industrial commodities as part of the 1963 stabilisation. The Italian government nationalised the power industry, and introduced new profits taxes and import deterrents as well as vastly stepping up its involvement in its long-standing efforts to industrialise the Mezzogiorno. Even the United States offered such phenomena as presidential interventions on the price of steel, restrictions on overseas investment, and an attempt to operate a wages policy.

Future historians may well regard it as a curious coincidence that while this was happening, and while Britain was undergoing an increase in state intervention in industry unmatched in modern peace-time history, the communist nations were busy taking their first hesitant steps towards restoration of the profit motive and the market economy.

Britain's plunge into interventionism substantially pre-dated the Labour administrations of 1964 and 1966. As the nation moved from the post-Suez crisis through a brief boom into the 1961–62 crisis and then into obviously unsoundly based prosperity in 1964, the successors of Sir Winston Churchill and his 'set the people free' slogan, grasped with increasing haste and frequency for interventionist measures. It was Conservative Governments who introduced the concept of national economic planning—and disastrously tied public expenditure to the planned four per cent economic growth rate. It was Conservatives who demanded a 'pay pause', introduced an incomes policy (with little effect), and set up a quasi-official commission to pronounce on incomes questions. Conservatives similarly introduced measures to persuade or force industry to do what was deemed good for it in such fields as investment, resale price maintenance, and industrial training.

Nor did Conservative ministers refrain from direct and detailed intervention in individual sectors of industry. Mr Duncan Sandys, as Minister of Aviation, imposed a massive restructuring upon Britain's aircraft industry. Mr Enoch Powell, as Minister of Health, initiated the import of 'pirated' drugs for National Health Service hospitals.

The motor industry was cajoled into setting up plants in Scotland, Wales and on Merseyside to reduce regional employment disparities.

THE 1964 GENERAL ELECTION

The Conservatives' increasing espousal of interventionism has been regarded by some commentators as the old political process of stealing one's opponents' clothes. The Labour Party under Mr Hugh Gaitskell had argued, though without very consistent enthusiasm, for more planning and controls. Under its new leader, Mr Harold Wilson, demands for more intervention to secure faster growth and make British industry more efficient became increasingly strident as the 1964 General Election approached.

Both the Conservative and Labour leaders were appealing to what appeared to be a well-established current of public opinion.

By 1964 the idea of national economic planning had become 'consensus' politics. Mr Selwyn Lloyd, as Conservative Chancellor of the Exchequer, had set up the National Economic Development Council in July 1961, and its so-called National Plan (*Growth of the United Kingdom Economy to 1966*) had received considerable acclaim when it was published in March 1963. It was broadly acceptable to most shades of opinion. To the left, who had always advocated planning, it was a modest step forward, though there were natural demands for more 'teeth' and claims that if the economy was henceforth to be planned, Socialists were the proper people to do it. Conservatives found it convenient to assume that the four per cent growth rate would actually be achieved, and went so far as to plan public expenditure on this assumption. The uncommitted found even the possibility of four per cent growth attractive, while industry welcomed the Government's commitment to planning in the hope that it presaged more enlightened and expansionist economic policies.

Thus, in the space of a few years, the idea of central planning of the economy had lost the taint of bureaucratic socialism and become respectable. Though it involved more controversy and bitterness, the concept of incomes policy—reintroduced by Mr Selwyn Lloyd after a twelve-year gap since Sir Stafford Cripps' 'freeze'—also became consensus politics. Tories had always been prepared to accept that the main engine of inflation was trade-union negotiated wage increases outstripping growth of productivity, and therefore saw nothing too outrageous in the Government providing 'guiding lights' or referring pay problems to a National Incomes Commission. Labour and the trade unions bitterly attacked Mr Selwyn Lloyd's efforts, but eventually accepted that a Labour government might operate an incomes policy so long as the idea was dressed up in the euphemism 'planned growth of incomes'.

At the 1964 General Election voters were thus offered little apparent choice in basic economic policy. Whichever major party won, the economy was to be planned and an incomes policy was to be pursued. Both parties suggested that the whole process was to be voluntary.

There were, of course, differences in emphasis, which political spokesmen were at pains to stress. Labour also promised much more in the fields of technology ('the white-hot technical revolution') and price restraint than the Tories could with a record to defend, and it offered steel nationalisation, too, although many who otherwise supported the party's economic policies dismissed this as doctrinaire or irrelevant.

In addition, Labour promised 'fair' taxation. The main elements in this 'fairness' were to be some egalitarian attacks on evasion, capital gains, and profits from land speculation. Distinctions were to be drawn between those who earned money and those who 'made' it. Since the Conservatives had already introduced a capital gains tax and conceded that profits on land redevelopment sales should be taxed, they could hardly differ in principle from the opposition. Instead they suggested that Labour's proposals (including their planned social reforms) would mean rising taxation. Both Mr Wilson and Mr Callaghan, the Shadow Chancellor, gave assurances that 'over the life of a Parliament' there should be no rise in general levels of taxation. Four years later, with over £2,000 million added to the nation's tax bills, this must rank as either the most naïve or the most misleading assurance ever given by politicians, but at the time it no doubt seemed categorical enough to inspire confidence.

To the average voter, unsophisticated in economic matters, it must have seemed that both political parties were offering very similar remedies. He may well have reasoned that if national economic planning was really to be the answer to 'stop-go' and other familiar ailments, then Mr Wilson was a more credible practitioner than Sir Alec Douglas-Home.

THE 1966 GENERAL ELECTION

The General Election of March 1966, offered, perhaps, more real choice between economic policies. Labour had not, of course, delivered the promised stability or growth, but it had courageously and determinedly clung to office with what the experts had declared to be an unworkably tiny majority and had proceeded with much of its declared programme. It could reasonably claim that its inheritance had been disastrous, that it needed more time and a satisfactory majority.

It also pointed to the 1965 National Plan as evidence of 'goodies' to come. *In the next five years living standards for the individual and for the whole community will rise by twenty-five per cent, as we increase our production of goods and services*, declared the Manifesto.* Many economic forecasters disagreed and were suggesting that massive deflation must follow the Election and remove any remaining credibility from the Plan, but Labour spokesmen treated such suggestions with disdain. In fact, Mr Callaghan's May budget provided for a deflation of £240 million via the deferred Selective Employment Tax, while Mr Wilson's July 1966 measures were to add another £500 million of deflation. They were also to introduce legal sanctions for incomes policy.

All this, however, was in the future so far as the electors were concerned. Their choice was between Labour's National Plan, with the promised (beneficial) effects of such things as investment grants, licensing of inessential building, and the Industrial Reorganisation Corporation thrown in, and a somewhat ill-defined Conservative economic policy. The Conservatives avoided any kind of commitment to national economic planning, attacking it indirectly with calls for 'less talk and gimmickry'.† They promised more incentives and more competition, without being very specific about the details except in the sphere of trade union reform. They implicitly endorsed incomes policy, claiming that their *new economic programme* would *make a prices and incomes policy really effective.** In the event, of course, Labour easily won the Election with a majority of ninety-seven seats.

A RISING TIDE OF INTERVENTION

Throughout its period of office the Labour Government has amply fulfilled its implicit pledges to increase substantially State intervention in industry. While such factors are difficult to measure, it seems probable that the degree of intervention now practised is substantially greater than anything imposed upon industry in peace time since the

* Labour Party Manifesto 1966.
† Conservative Party Manifesto 1966.

industrial revolution, apart from the years immediately following 1945 when another Labour administration inherited and made full use of a massive apparatus of controls.

These interventionist policies and measures are described in considerable detail in Chapters 2 to 7. A quick conspectus, however, of the additional intervention imposed on the British economy during Labour's term of office can be obtained simply by looking at the main headings under which the Government has sought to impose its theories and wishes.

These include:

New Ministries with interventionist powers—
The Department of Economic Affairs, Ministry of Technology, the Department of Employment and Productivity.

New Interventionist Taxes—
The Import Surcharge, Corporation Tax, Capital Gains Tax, Close Company Penalties, Selective Employment Tax, the Imports Deposit Scheme.

Other Fiscal Measures—
Export Rebate, Investment Grants, Controls on Overseas Investment.

Tax Regulation of the Economy—
The use of soaring taxes to control consumers' expenditure.

Prices and Incomes Policy—
Including compulsory controls of prices, wages, and dividends.

Negative Regional Development Restrictions—
Tougher rules on Industrial Development Certificates, Building Licences, and restriction on office building.

Increasing Regional Inducements—
Investment Grant Premiums, SET Differentials, Regional Employment Premiums.

New Interventionist Agencies—
The Prices and Incomes Board, the Industrial Re-organisation Corporation.

Steel Nationalisation.

The Transport Act—
    Including compulsory powers for direction of freight traffic and a
    free hand for nationalised industries.

These headings do not cover all the measures of intervention into
industry which Labour has undertaken, nor is it claimed that
Chapters 2 to 7 contain a completely comprehensive account of the
total of intervention in industry which has occurred during the
period under study. Quite apart from the massive degree of intervention for which they have taken statutory powers, Labour ministers
have practised a very high degree of personal ad hoc intervention in
industry, much of it involving State funds or State commitments to
support enterprises of various kinds. What is important, so far as
this book is concerned, is not to chronicle every detail of State intervention in industry but to identify the main lines of intervention and
to establish what success, if any, they have achieved.

EVALUATION OF INTERVENTION

It is a matter of stark fact that by the end of 1968 this policy of
massive and detailed intervention had not produced the major
improvement in Britain's economic situation which was so confi-
dently predicted in 1964. On any major count—the balance of payments, economic growth, capital investment, personal living standards—Labour's four years of office had produced slower progress
or a consistently worse outcome than the average level of achievement during their predecessors' thirteen years of power. While 1968
produced the period's only substantial upsurge in industrial output
and productivity, this owed more to devaluation and a spectacular
rise in world trade than to any of the interventionist policies deliberately adopted by the Government.

It would be unduly simplistic to deduce from this unhappy
economic record that intervention in industry has failed, or, indeed,
made matters worse than they would otherwise have been; it can
equally well be argued that our economic experience would have been
even more traumatic if Labour had not pressed on with the measures
which it claims to be modernising and restructuring industry. Such
conflicting claims can only be reasonably assessed by a detailed study
of what has been done in the field of intervention in industry during
the past five years and an objective attempt to evaluate the results of
this intervention to date.

Such a study inevitably takes us into difficult roles of cause and
effect. Such relationships are rarely very clear in economic matters.
A modern market economy is an immensely complicated mechanism
and interference at any one point can cause a chain of reactions far

beyond those anticipated. Intervention can similarly bring not only the effect which was expected, but a variety of side effects which may or may not be welcome. Economic matters are further complicated by the fact that they produce psychological and emotive reactions.

These may not be strictly rational, but they nevertheless cause people to act in ways which affect further economic events. For better or for worse intervention in industry, particularly of a negative or compulsory or discriminatory nature, produces emotional reactions which may well frustrate or distort the original purposes of the intervention.

Another complication in economic investigation lies in the fact that it is usually impossible to predict with precision the effects of a given course of action in advance of trying it out. It is thus easy to ascertain that a particular line of policy has failed to fulfil its objectives but this does not make it certain that some alternative policy would necessarily have done better. In economic matters it is impossible to put back the clock and start again. None of this, of course, prevents economists whose policies were not adopted from asserting that they would have done the trick where others failed!

Our approach to these difficult matters is essentially pragmatic. In the first part of this book we chronicle and examine the measures of intervention which the Government actually adopted during the period from 15 October, 1964, to the end of 1968. We examine the aims of each particular measure, where possible as explained by those who introduced it. In the second part of this book we endeavour to trace the effects of each of the major groups of interventionist measures introduced during the period, by reference to the relevant statistics and to the statements of informed commentators on industrial progress following intervention, Since the effects of intervention may well require considerable time to manifest themselves we also attempt to evaluate the future consequences of the continuance of some of the present policies of intervention.

It would be idle to expect a study such as this to produce some conclusive case for or against all industrial intervention. The best we can hope for in general terms is some indication as to whether a massive increase in intervention, such as we have witnessed during the last five years is in overall terms likely to produce beneficial or adverse effects on the British economy. Beyond this, and irrespective of the general verdict, one would expect to find that certain forms of intervention appear to produce beneficial results, while others appear to do more harm than good. It is important for future policy making that these particular types should be identified as conclusively as possible.

14 STATE INTERVENTION IN BRITISH INDUSTRY 1964–68

The performance of British industry is of crucial importance to the aspirations of every citizen. If governments are to intervene in industrial policies and operations, or to refrain rigorously from intervening, it is essential that their decision should be made on the basis of as much fact as can be elucidated, and not just on the basis of economic theorising or political dogma.

CHAPTER TWO

New ministries of intervention

One of the most important factors in Labour's narrow General Election victory in 1964 was the promise it appeared to offer for remedying the economic troubles which had for so long beset the nation.

The heart of these remedies was planning. The Party's 1964 General Election Manifesto had proclaimed: *The aims are simple enough: we want full employment; a faster rate of industrial expansion; a sensible distribution of industry throughout the country; an end to the present chaos in traffic and transport; a brake on rising prices and a solution to our balance of payments problems. As the past thirteen years have shown, none of these aims will be achieved by leaving the economy to look after itself. They will only be secured by a deliberate and massive effort to modernise the economy; to change its structure and to develop with all possible speed the advanced technology and the new science-based industries with which our future lies. In short they will only be achieved by Socialist planning.*

As the above quotation suggests, Labour had also promised the nation a kind of bonus in 'the white-hot technical revolution'. This was to be achieved by establishing new industries 'either by public enterprise or in partnership with private industry'; by the use of research and development contracts in the field of civil production: and by ministerial effort 'to guide and stimulate a major national effort to bring advanced technology and new processes into industry'.

The keys to this promised transformation of the economy and of British industry were to be two new ministries. The Ministry of Economic Affairs (as it was called in the Manifesto) would have the duty of formulating, with both sides of industry, a national economic plan and would frame the broad strategy for increasing investment, expanding exports and replacing inessential imports. The Ministry of Technology would, of course, spearhead the promised 'technical revolution'.

DEPARTMENT OF ECONOMIC AFFAIRS

The formation of the Department of Economic Affairs, with Mr

George Brown as First Secretary of State and Secretary of State for Economic Affairs, was announced within hours of Mr Wilson taking office as Prime Minister. The staff of the Department was thereafter assembled at high speed. Labour had inherited a fairly substantial planning apparatus in the National Economic Development Council. One of the DEA's first actions was to take over the Economic Planning section of NEDC, under Sir Donald MacDougall, and virtually its entire staff. Further sections of the Department were staffed by direct cannibalisation of existing Treasury departments. The Industrial Policies Department was set up through the recruitment of a distinguished industrialist, Mr H. F. R. Catherwood (seconded from his appointment as Managing Director of British Aluminium) and the recruitment or secondment of a number of industrial advisers from industry and journalism. The organisation of the Department, as it developed under Mr George Brown, is shown in the chart on page 17, which also gives an excellent indication of the functions for which it was responsible.

The functions of the new ministry, and its priorities, were outlined and elaborated by the First Secretary in statements to the House of Commons on 4 November and 10 December 1964. As expected one of the new ministry's priorities was to be preparation of the promised national plan. Another was to be formulation and adoption of a prices and incomes policy in collaboration with both sides of industry. The third priority was regional planning, with the establishment of Regional Economic Planning Boards and Councils in most parts of the country. Developments in the fields of prices and incomes policy and regional policy are considered in detail in further chapters in this book (Chapters 4 and 5). Our concern here is to trace the progress of the DEA in the field of national planning and the co-ordination of economic policy, in its pursuit of policies intended to promote industrial efficiency and in its relations with NEDC and the Economic Development Committees.

In fact, little needs to be said about the Department's achievements in co-ordinating economic policy, for in practical terms they were minimal. At no time did the DEA ever attain the 'overlordship' of the British economy which Labour intellectuals had assigned to it in their pre-election theorising. According to such theories, the hitherto preponderant influence of the Treasury, with its alleged over-caution constantly thwarting economic growth, would be drastically diminished once a Department of Economic Affairs was set up. The Department would make the major decisions, according to an expansionist long-term strategy, leaving the Treasury with only the short-term role of office of the Budget.

It is doubtful whether the Prime Minister ever wholly accepted this

DEPARTMENT OF ECONOMIC AFFAIRS 1965

FIRST SECRETARY OF STATE
AND SECRETARY OF STATE FOR ECONOMIC AFFAIRS
Rt Hon. George Brown, MP

MINISTER OF STATE
Mr A. Albu, MP

PARLIAMENTARY UNDER-SECRETARIES
Mr M. A. Foley, MP
Mr W. T. Rodgers, MP

PERMANENT UNDER-SECRETARY OF STATE
Sir Eric Roll

ECONOMIC CO-ORDINATION
Mr D. A. V. Allen

INFORMATION DIVISION
Mr J. D. Groves

ECONOMIC PLANNING
Sir Donald MacDougall

ECONOMIC PLANNING
Mr J. A. Jukes

REGIONAL POLICY
Mr A. W. Peterson

REGIONAL PHYSICAL PLANNING, LAND USE, TRANSPORT
Mr J. E. Beddoe

REGIONAL ECONOMIC PLANNING, INDUSTRY, EMPLOYMENT
Mr R. R. D. McIntosh

INDUSTRIAL POLICIES
Mr H. F. R. Catherwood

INDUSTRIAL MATTERS, PROMOTION OF INDUSTRIAL EFFICIENCY
Mr P. E. Thornton

(Industrial Advisers)
Dr J. A. Berriman
Mr A. C. H. Cairns
Mr M. Shanks
Mr I. J. Young

EXTERNAL RELATIONS
Mr W. A. Nield

GROWTH, INCOMES AND PRICES POLICY
Mr E. W. Maude

PUBLIC EXPENDITURE
Mr D. O. Henley

ESTABLISHMENTS AND FINANCE
Mr I. F. Hudson

This chart sets out the broad functional grouping of the senior administrative and professional staff of the Department. It does not reflect the hierarchical ranking of individual officers.

Source: DEA Progress Report No. 1, January 1965

B

idea of DEA 'overlordship', but in any case the Government's progress from one short-term crisis to another made long-term theorising about the economy increasingly irrelevant. Even when Mr Brown held power at the DEA and was nominally No. 2 in the power structure, most of the crucial decisions about the economy were made in the Treasury, with the Department holding only such forlorn babies as the Mark I, wholly voluntary incomes policy. Once the July 1966 'stop' had been imposed in the teeth of Mr Brown's opposition, all pretence of DEA co-ordination of economic policy was abandoned.

One result of the formation of the Department was a considerable change in the status and functioning of the National Economic Development Council. As we have seen, the economic planning function was entirely subsumed into the new ministry. The new First Secretary of State replaced the Chancellor of the Exchequer as Chairman and government representation on the Council was increased from three to five by bringing in the Minister of Technology and a new senior official, the chief Industrial Adviser of the DEA.

THE NATIONAL PLAN

It is not unfair to regard national economic planning as the element which Labour regarded as crucial to its success when it took office. This can be readily confirmed by reference to its 1964 General Election Manifesto, and by the appointment of the Deputy Leader of the party to the newly created DEA. The Manifesto recognised that there would be a need for what it called 'short-term priority' in closing the trade gap, and suggested a number of detailed measures which it would adopt. These, however, were only seen as preliminaries to reaping the fruits of the planning exercise. The Manifesto stated: *But in the long run a satisfactory trade balance will depend upon carrying out Labour's overall plan to revitalise and modernise the whole economy. It will depend upon maintaining a steady and vigorous programme of long-term expansion.*

In early statements on the work of the DEA considerable emphasis was laid upon the initial steps being taken to prepare the National Plan. In January 1965, Mr George Brown summed up the aims in his Department's first progress report: *DEA is now preparing a general plan for Britain's economic development. Both sides of industry are being fully consulted through the National Economic Development Committees and the Industrial Councils. The maximum use is being made of advanced economic techniques. An outline will be published in the spring, and the full plan in the summer.*

The aim will be to raise productivity—to reach the four per cent *growth target as soon as possible—and to sharpen Britain's competitive ability. The Government will treat the Plan not as a forecast of what might happen if things go right, but as a commitment and a blueprint for action. Beyond the public sector, the Plan will be a guide for a truly national effort. Industry will know much more about its opportunities than ever before, and decisions should be more profitable to everyone concerned.**

What in fact subsequently happened to the Plan—its appearance in September 1965, to the full blast of the publicity machines of the Government and the Labour Party, its use as an election aid in the 1966 General Election, and its abandonment four months later in the July 1966 special measures—constituted one of the more grandiose non-events in British economic history. It may be argued that the sequence of events involved in the Plan's preparation and its subsequent collapse is sufficiently well known to warrant no further attention. Since, however, national economic planning was regarded by the Labour Party itself, and by many non-committed people, both in industry and among the general public, as offering substantial help in improving our economic performance, it is desirable that we should examine what was involved in the preparation of this abortive plan and in its subsequent abandonment, so that we can profit from whatever lessons may emerge.

A full, if critical account of the preparation of the National Plan, by a former Treasury planner, was given in *The National Plan—a Preliminary Assessment*, by John Brunner in 1965.† The steps essentially involved were, first, a political decision on the growth rate to be pursued. The four per cent per annum compound adopted by NEDC under the Conservatives was thought to be too high, with a figure nearer to three and a half per cent per annum as probably the most realistic and practicable. This was thought to be uninspiring, so the eventual political compromise was to run the plan from the year prior to its preparation, 1964, through to 1970. A twenty-five per cent growth over the six-year period gives a compound rate of 3·8 per cent per annum. This was thought to be not impossibly high, so twenty-five per cent in six years became the target.

This particular political judgment having been made, a second judgment was required on how the putative gains from the planning exercise should be divided among the various components of final demand. The table on page 20 shows the division which the Plan expected.

The next stage of preparation of the Plan was the industrial questionnaire. Within the frame-work of a number of general

* DEA Progress Report No. 1, January 1965.
† Institute of Economic Affairs, Eaton Paper No. 4.

assumptions postulated by the DEA—that GDP would increase by
a quarter between 1964 and 1970, that exports would have to increase
up to twice as fast as in the past, that the labour force would grow
by only one and a half per cent by 1970, and that 1970 would be 'an
average year with overseas markets in an average state'—industrial
companies were asked to forecast their output, investment, employment, etc., over the plan period.

The third stage of the planning exercise was generally known as
'mutual adjustment'. The explanatory memorandum accompanying
the questionnaire explained that information was being sought 'to

DIVISION OF ANTICIPATED NATIONAL PLAN GROWTH

Use of resources

	1964	Increase 1964–70	
	£ million, 1964 prices	£ million, 1964 prices (round numbers)	Percentage
Gross national product	32,847	8,210	25
Balance of trade in goods and ser- vices, and net investment income from abroad*	−226	500	..
Investment:			
Manufacturing and construction	1,351	740	55
Other private industries and ser- vices	1,298	320	25
Nationalised industries	1,145	345	30
Stockbuilding	526	5	..
Housing	1,209	385	32
Roads†	194	145	74
Other public services	546	270	50
Transfer costs of land and building	59	5	..
Defence‡	1,930	115	6
Consumption:			
Social and other public services	3,481	925	27
Personal	21,334	4,455	21

* This differs from the balance of payments on current account by the amount
of net transfers abroad.

† New road works and major road improvements; excluding minor improvements and maintenance expenditure, and purchases of land.

‡ These figures cover current military defence expenditure on goods and services
on the definitions used in the statistics of National Income and Expenditure
published by the Central Statistical Office; the coverage is somewhat wider than
that used for the Defence Budget. The 1970 figure is consistent with the Defence
Budget at constant prices being limited to a total equivalent to that provided for
in the Estimates for 1964–65, i.e. £2,000 million.

Source: National Plan 1965

give some guide to the amount of revision of firms' existing plans which will be required to bring them into line with the National Plan'. What in effect followed the return of the questionnaires was an exhaustive analysis within the DEA and various consultant bodies of the numerous apparently irreconcilable intentions which the questionnaires had revealed. Following this analysis came a good deal of contact between industry and the Department which the DEA progress report described as *further consultations with the industries who have completed the returns in order to reduce any inconsistencies and imbalances by mutual agreement*. It seems certain, in fact, some of this 'mutual agreement' consisted of industrialists reluctantly accepting figures which the DEA thought probable or desirable, rather than the insertion of what industry regarded as its own realistic plans.

Coincidental with the discussion with industry, the DEA planners were involved in a series of mathematical readjustments by successive approximation using the technique known as 'iterative procedures' to arrive at internal consistency and to smooth out apparent contradictions.

The final stage of the exercise was, of course, the preparation of the final report and the planning of the publicity attached to its launching.

This is a highly condensed account of what was involved in the National Plan exercise, but it does indicate some of the weaknesses inherent in the technique and it also indicates something of the cost of preparation. One of the obvious weaknesses is the fact that the planners themselves fix the growth target and then invite industry to make a series of detailed projections on the assumption that the target will be fulfilled. No doubt some informed thought and study is given to determination of the target, but if the planners choose a growth rate which is substantially different from that assumed by the majority of industrialists then the exercise moves into a game of theoretical guess-work so far as industry is concerned. Once this factor intervenes, the input of information into the plan becomes increasingly unreliable. For example, an unrealistically high target specifically invites industry to assume higher demand elasticities and consequently higher investment expenditure than experience and its own studies have led it to expect.

Since, however, the planners can honestly claim that industry has supplied the information on which the plan is based, it is only a short step to the claim that the plan itself is 'endorsed by industry' and thus forms a commitment on the part of industrialists. Michael Shanks* has made the point that the 1965 National Plan was essen-

* *The Times*, 13 January 1969.

tially a Government plan *sold to the CBI and TUC by George Brown at the last minute*. He goes on to explain vividly that: *The manner in which it was sold to the CBI members of the Neddy Council—in an all-night session in Sir Frank Kearton's house in the wilds of Buckinghamshire, where Mr Brown appeared as an uninvited guest after midnight—has continued to rankle. Rightly or wrongly, the CBI leaders feel they were hustled into endorsing what was almost a phony prospectus, and don't intend to get caught again.*

THE END OF THE PLAN

Despite the massive publicity with which the Plan was launched, which virtually ensured a good initial press, there was no shortage of immediate criticisms. What most economists doubted were the balance of payments projections on which the Plan hinged. Mr George Brown had himself stressed the priority which had to be given to achievement of external balance in his foreword to the Plan. In the view of the more percipient critics the Plan's projections on external trade were highly optimistic. With a deficit in prospect for 1965, and few obvious reasons to expect any great improvement in the external situation in 1966, it is probably fair to say that expert opinion never regarded the Plan as feasible from the moment of its publication.

During the next ten months criticisms that the Plan was being steadily invalidated by lack of improvement in the balance of payments situation were repeated frequently, and in mounting chorus, and were stridently denied by Government spokesmen. By the time of the General Election in March 1966 the majority of economic opinion was forecasting that 'stop' measures would be necessary either in the budget which would speedily follow the election, or later in the year. Labour Party spokesmen found it convenient to ignore these predictions and to assume during the election campaign that the Plan's targets would be met.

In the event, Mr Callaghan introduced a deflationary Budget in May 1966, but one with a delayed impact since one of its major measures—the introduction of Selective Employment Tax—was not to take effect until September. What followed was a rapidly worsening balance of payments situation, a run on sterling, and the introduction of Mr Wilson's crisis measures on 20 July 1966.

The estimated effect of these measures was to reduce demand in the home economy by more than £500 million. At the same time a 'freeze' was to be applied to prices and incomes for six months, to be followed by a further six months of 'severe restraint'. Among the measures introduced were a ten per cent surcharge on surtax and a reduction from £100,000 to £50,000 in the cost limit making building projects subject to control. The specific intention of this extension of building control was to defer an increasing amount of private construction.

Following the announcement of these measures, there was a good deal of coyness on the part of Government spokesmen in admitting that the National Plan was dead. The DEA for example commented :* *The cut-back in the expansion of the economy which the measures imply means that a twenty-five per cent growth in output* 1964–70 *is no longer attainable: it is therefore necessary to reconsider the figuring of the Plan and the time scale.* From this and other events it is clear that for a while the Government toyed with the idea of dealing with the situation by producing a revised version of the Plan.

In November 1966, the First Secretary—now Mr Michael Stewart —announced that after further consultations with NEDC he had decided not to publish a review of progress on the Plan in 1966, but would consult further with the Council and other organisations to determine the kind of planning operation that would be most effective in future in achieving the objects of growth. This can, perhaps, be regarded as official recognition of the demise of the Plan.

Despite the brief life of this grandiose National Plan (and the even briefer period in which it was taken seriously) vestiges of its influence still linger on. Even as late as the end of 1968 Treasury defenders of charges of excessive public spending were still replying to critics with statements that public expenditure had not risen above the National Plan projections. This looks like a very damaging admission that the invalidated assumptions of the Plan were still influencing official action in a way which, in the view of many critics, constitutes a major danger to improvement of the economic situation.

THE PLAN MARK III

The rapid collapse of the 1965 National Plan naturally led to a substantial loss of public credibility in the whole idea of economic planning. It also led to substantially diminished prestige for the Department of Economic Affairs. Some loss in the influence of the Department was in any case inevitable when the dynamic Mr George Brown, after toying with the idea of resignation from the Government at the abandonment of the growth idea implicit in the July 1966 measures, moved to the Foreign Office and was succeeded by a much less colourful personality, Mr Michael Stewart. The Department received further blows to its influence in the summer of 1967 when the Prime Minister took over nominal responsibility for Economic Affairs and the office of Secretary of State at the DEA was filled by a relatively junior Minister, Mr Peter Shore. To some critics, the last reason for the existence of the Department disappeared when

* DEA Progress Report No. 19, August 1966.

responsibility for the prices and incomes policy was shifted to the newly created Department of Employment and Productivity.

Despite these setbacks, planning enthusiasts within the Department, and within the NED office, kept plugging away with the idea that some new kind of national planning exercise was desirable. This was to be a very different kind of plan, not geared to a single central target, but would project the implications of a range of growth rates.

In November 1968 the Secretary of State for Economic Affairs told the NEDC that a working draft of the new Plan would be circulated to Council members by the end of the month, and would be the subject of a special meeting to be held on 15 December at Chequers. The main news that emerged from the Chequers meeting was of massive disagreement between trade union representatives serving on NEDC and the Government and industry representatives over the growth rate the Plan assumed the nation could sustain. The TUC were arguing for a six per cent growth rate, while the growth rate embodied in the draft document and generally accepted as reasonable by industry and the Government, was of the order of three to three and a quarter per cent.

This was one of the most dramatic of dissensions over the new Plan. Among the others were arguments over whether the CBI would endorse it on behalf of industry, on the timing of publication of the Plan if it were to be adopted, and apparently divided views within the Government itself on whether there was any value in publishing a further Plan—particularly one which did not have the propaganda value of an ambitious central growth target.

In the event, the new projections—cautiously described as 'a planning document', not a plan—were published in February 1969 as a Green Paper under the title 'The Task Ahead'. What effect, if any, this document will have on the economic life of the nation is obscure at the time of writing.

OTHER ACTIVITIES OF THE DEA

The main functions of the Department of Economic Affairs, apart from its central planning role, have been the formulation and operation of the prices and incomes policy (until responsibility was transferred to the DEP in April 1968) and regional planning. These are dealt with in Chapters 4 and 5.

The other main function which the Department has carried out during its years of existence has been to operate the Industrial Advisory Service, mostly through its involvement in the work of the 'little Neddies'. Labour inherited the 'little Neddy' concept and nine committees from the Conservative Administration. These have now multiplied to twenty-one.

The DEA's main and continuing contact with industry comes through the presence of members of its Industrial Advisory staff on the 'little Neddy' committees. This position gives the Department a channel to influence individual industries in the way the Government wishes, and it also, of course, provides industry with a means of making known its detailed views to the Government. The main visible product of the 'little Neddy' system is a substantial output of reports covering such matters as market prospects, exports and imports, investment intentions, etc., in each of the industries represented by a 'little Neddy'. Some of these reports have drawn attention to management techniques which the industries concerned could with advantage use to greater intensity. One of the more novel approaches has been the publication by the clothing industry EDC of a series of profitability 'league tables' intended to stimulate the less profitable companies in the industry to greater efforts.

It is difficult to summarise the effects of the 'little Neddy' system, or to assess its value, if only because the individual committees vary considerably in vigour and quality of chairmanship and membership. The majority of industrialists probably regard them as moderately useful bodies, permitting the discussion of the major problems of industry between businessmen, trade unions and Government representatives in an objective and non-partisan atmosphere. There are, however, some reservations about the amount of time they take up (see Chapter 13) while another fairly common complaint concerns the apparent indifference of the Government to the advice given to it by the 'little Neddies'. A particular example here is the motor industry's plea for a stable home market as an essential base for exports: despite the EDC's strong endorsement of this plea, the industry's home market was either deliberately or coincidentally subjected to massive contractions in the fiscal measures imposed in the 1968 Budget and then again in the measures adopted in November.

Apart from its continuing preoccupations, the DEA has been involved in a number of individual sorties in industrial intervention. The best known and most controversial of these was the Department's rescue of the Fairfield shipyard in 1965. The essence of the controversy was the use of Government money to keep going a single shipyard in competition with other private enterprise yards which enjoyed no such sponsorship. The initial justification for the venture was that 5,000 jobs were involved, but Fairfields was thereafter made a centre for some interesting experiments in labour relations and productivity measures. At the time of the yard's merger into the Upper Clyde consortium the generally accepted verdict on these experiments was 'not proven'.

Other measures devised or sponsored by the Department of

Economic Affairs include the Industrial Reorganisation Corporation
and the Industrial Expansion Act, which are considered in Chapters
6 and 7.

MINISTRY OF TECHNOLOGY

If we are to get a dynamic and expanding economy the 1964 Labour
Party Manifesto declared, *it is essential that new and effective ways
are found for injecting modern technology into our industries.* This was
a modestly phrased statement of the Party's aims. In the speeches of
its spokesmen, particularly Mr Harold Wilson, much more dramatic
claims had been made about the potential impact of modern technology, and a 'white-hot technical revolution' had been promised.

The implication behind these claims and promises, was, of course,
that Britain had lagged in the application and commercial exploitation of technological advance. This is not an easy proposition to
measure. What can be established is that the nation, both prior to
1964 and since, has spent more on research and development per head
of population, than any of its competitors among the main industrial
nations, except the United States, without achieving an economic
growth rate comparable with that of its competitors. A high proportion of military research expenditure (around forty per cent) in the
British R & D effort does something to explain the apparent lack of
industrial pay off, but a high rate of R & D spending combined with
a low rate of economic growth at least provides some presumptive
evidence that the industrial potential of technology has not been
properly exploited. The proposition was certainly widely accepted
at the time of the 1964 General Election, and Labour's promise of
vigorous action to remedy the situation constituted a powerful
attraction, especially in intellectual circles.

The spearhead for the revolution was to be a new Ministry of
Technology. On the morrow of the General Election, Mr Wilson
announced the setting up of the new ministry and the somewhat
controversial appointment of Mr Frank Cousins, the Left wing
General Secretary of the Transport and General Workers' Union,
as Britain's first Minister of Technology.

Labour had never made it very clear quite how the promised
revolution was to be effected. Spokesmen had talked of increasing
use of research and development contracts in the civil field to stimulate new advance, and of the setting up of new industries, either by
public enterprise, or in partnership with private firms, to exploit
them. Most questions on how the technological revolution was to be
brought about, were, however, dealt with by Labour spokesmen by
confident reiteration of assurances that the new Ministry of Technology would devise ways and means. This was an interesting

example of the general theme so frequently recurrent in Labour's philosophy, that a suitable body of experts in Whitehall could somehow transform the performance of British industry.

In the event, the obvious effect of creation of the Ministry of Technology has been the reshuffling of a vast array of already existing Government departments, agencies, and research establishments, to bring them under the direction of a single powerful minister. Among those thus reshuffled are the old Department of Scientific and Industrial Research, the Ministry of Aviation, some elements from the Board of Trade and the Ministry of Defence, and the former separate service ministries. The regrouping has made the Ministry one of the largest single employers of scientific labour in Western Europe, and has been accompanied by efforts to harness the extremely diverse range of activities involved to some reasonably consistent industrial objectives, and to securing substantially more collaboration between Government research and development activities and private industry. This effort is clearly desirable, since the enlarged Ministry by February 1967 was employing 36,500 people and spending about £750,000,000 annually.

The bulk of this huge staff is concentrated in the research group which includes ten former DSIR research stations, seven Ministry of Aviation R & D establishments, the Atomic Energy Authority, forty-seven industrial research associations, and the National Research Development Corporation; and in the Aviation Group which, in the words of the Ministry's Permanent Secretary:* *organises the development and procurement of aircraft and other defence equipment; does the same for some civil aircraft (of which much the most significant is the Concorde); and handles the Government's relationship with the aircraft industry, and in particular the reorganisation of the industry now under negotiation.*

SPONSORSHIP

Regrouping all these existing activities has certain potential value, but it was clearly unlikely to bring about changes which could conceivably be described as revolutionary. Much more was hoped for from the 'sponsorship' function of the Ministry. Under this concept the Ministry seeks 'to foster the economic and technological development and competitive power of the engineering industry in its widest sense'.†

The sponsorship function in fact covers five industry divisions: Electronics; Computers; Machine tools and manufacturing machinery; Vehicles and mechanical engineering; Shipbuilding, electrical

* Sir Richard Clarke, *New Technology* No. 2, February 1967.
† Sir Richard Clarke, *New Technology* No. 14, February 1968.

and process plant. In addition the Aviation Group, already referred to, can be regarded as sponsoring the aircraft industry.

What does 'sponsorship' involve? An informative brief account was given by the Permanent Secretary as part of a lecture in February 1968:* *The job of the industry divisions is to know their industries. They deal with industries' problems as they come up—the impact of Government economic measures, such as hire-purchase regulations; help to firms with export problems; hearing from firms and trade associations where the shoe pinches; and telling them where the shoe pinches from the Government's point of view. This provides the communication link between the industries and the Government. Second only to this communication function is the divisions' duty to do what they can to strengthen the industries' technology and competitive power. We have a large variety of projects of this kind under way. These may be to develop some new machine or technique. The patterns cover a very wide range—surveys of sectors of industry, in comparison with foreign countries; evolution of standard systems of costing; strengthening technical information services, and so on. There is usually a contract between the Department and a firm, or a group of firms, or an industrial research association, or a university, or a combination of these, often worked out in collaboration with the Department's research establishments (or AEA), and providing for a sharing of the cost. This reinforces another source of funds for new R & D—the National Research Development Corporation, which takes proposals from industry which carry a more clearly measurable financial return. The Department's largest operations of this constructive kind are in advanced machine tools (notably numerically-controlled machine tools), advanced computer techniques, microelectronics, scientific instruments. Some of these schemes, covering a large number of individual contracts, involve expenditure of as much as £5 million. But there are a lot of small cases of, say £20,000 or less each; and the results spread beyond the individual firm. The Government component enables industry itself to carry out schemes of modernisation that it would not otherwise be able to do.*

THE SERVICE DIVISIONS

In addition to its sponsorship and research functions, the Ministry has developed five divisions dealing with particular functions over the whole of the engineering industry and beyond. One division is concerned with standardisation, another with information and intelligence, and a third with economics and statistics.

One of the best known of the service divisions is that which deals with productivity services, exports, and international technological

* Sir Richard Clarke, *New Technology* No. 14, February 1968.

collaboration. From within this division has been developed a wide and diverse range of services—advisory and propaganda—intended to help industrialists to solve productivity problems and move on to more advanced methods of manufacture and management. The July 1968 issue of *New Technology*, the Ministry's monthly broadsheet, listed and explained over twenty such services. These are as follows:

Industrial Liaison Centres
Sixty-seven centres based on colleges of tehnology and universities provide a local information and liaison service, particularly for smaller firms, to help them make greater use of existing scientific and technological knowledge and sources of assistance.

Production Engineering Advisory Service
A regional mobile service operated by the Production Engineering Research Association for the engineering and allied industries. It provides technical advice, training and assistance in all aspects of production engineering.

Low Cost Automation Centres
Some colleges of technology and universities have set up centres to provide instruction, demonstrations and advice for smaller firms on inexpensive automatic control techniques.

Numerical Control Advisory and Demonstration Service
The service helps firms to assess the benefits of introducing NC equipment, and advises on the selection of NC machine tools. Programming, machining trials, demonstrations using a firm's own components, and training courses are features of the service.

Central Unit for Scientific Photography
An advisory and consultancy service on the application of photographic techniques to the solution of scientific, technological and production problems.

Industrial Applications Unit
This unit is the contact point between industry and the Royal Radar Establishment for advice on the whole range of electronics and associated equipment, and in particular micro-electronics, new components and electronic materials.

Interlab
The Interlab scheme aims to develop regional collaboration in research by enabling people working in different laboratories to share their experience and facilities.

SIRAID
The British Scientific Instrument Research Association operates an information and consultancy service on instrumentation, automation and associated problems in materials and engineering.

National Computing Centre
The centre was set up to accelerate the introduction and use of computers and provides an advisory service on data processing, computing, and computers. It also offers advice and training in systems analysis and programming techniques.

Productivity Services Based on UKAEA Establishments
A number of services have been established to make available to industry the expertise within the UKAEA.

Non-Destructive Testing Centre
The centre's aim is to assist industry to improve the quality and reliability of its products by the use of non-destructive testing techniques. The centre can undertake sponsored work for industry.

Ceramic Centre
An advisory and consultancy service on the fabrication, testing and use of ceramic materials.

Materials Technology Bureau
An advisory and consultancy service is provided on all aspects of materials technology, especially the use of new materials and of conventional materials in exacting conditions.

APACE
The Aldermaston Project for the Application of Computers to Engineering assists industry to gain experience in the application of computer aids to engineering design, planning and production.

National Centre for Tribology
The centre specialises in lubrication, friction and wear problems encountered under adverse conditions. It operates a consultancy service and undertakes research and development programmes on specific problems.

Advisory Centre on Isotopes
The Wantage Research Laboratory carries out R and D into the industrial use of radioactive isotopes and ionising radiations, and offers advice, information and practical services.

University Industrial Units
These units, sponsored by the Ministry, provide commercial consultancy and development services in industry.

Industrial Unit of Tribology, Leeds
This unit, based at the University of Leeds, will advise on all aspects of lubrication, friction and wear problems with particular emphasis on bearing design.

Industrial Unit of Tribology, Swansea
This unit, based at the University College of Swansea, will advise on lubrication problems in industrial environments, including the selection and design of bearings, seals and other components involving surfaces in relative motion.

Industrial Development Unit
The University College of North Wales will offer a service to industry in instrumentation and control engineering, and is equipped to undertake development to the prototype stage.

Centre for Industrial Innovation
A development and consultancy service is provided by the University of Strathclyde to cover electronics, physics, chemistry, food science and management sciences. Facilities are available for the design, development and manufacture of prototypes to industrial requirements.

Cranfield Unit for Precision Engineering
The Unit is part of the College of Aeronautics and carries out research into the methods of design and manufacture of high precision equipment with the aim of improving quality and reducing costs.

Source—'New Technology' (Ministry of Technology)

A fifth division deals with general industrial problems, such as industrial structure, mergers, prices, effects of public procurement, the problems of the engineering profession, and so on. The activities of this division, particularly in so far as they have led to interference through the Industrial Reorganisation Corporation, have involved the Ministry in some of its more controversial functions.

The spectrum of activities covered by the Ministry is so huge that it is difficult to select from it those which could be expected to have a distinctive impact on technology in Britain. As we have seen, much of the activity embraced by the new Ministry was already in existence, and a great deal which has subsequently happened under the aegis of the Ministry, including the dispensing of Government aid to ailing technological industries, would doubtless have happened irrespective of the Ministry's creation. What is perhaps most distinctive about the activities of Mintech is the productivity advisory services and other measures to popularise and speed the adoption of the most up to date technology. This range of activities includes the pre-production order scheme and facilities for enabling companies to try new machines at little cost or risk. Another relatively ambitious and imaginative venture has been the setting up of the National Computing Centre, intended to make it as easy and cheap as possible for companies to use the electronic computer. Contractual arrangements for research and development work, partly financed by the Government, have also been a distinctive field of operation for the new Ministry, particularly in process automation projects.

Another role which has devolved upon the Ministry has been international collaboration on research and development. The fruits here have not been especially large in terms of joint projects undertaken, but the Ministry has helped the Government to formulate a policy for technological collaboration with European nations, which is probably a great deal more ambitious than those of the Governments of the European Economic Community.

THE DEPARTMENT OF EMPLOYMENT AND PRODUCTIVITY

Under the Labour Government the Ministry of Labour for some three and a half years continued to fulfil virtually the same role which had been allotted to it under previous administrations. Primary responsibility for the incomes side of prices and incomes policy rested with the newly created Department of Economic Affairs, and so also did responsibility for policy measures to improve labour productivity.

A major reshuffle of Government responsibilities took place in April 1968 when the Ministry of Labour was transformed into the new Department of Employment and Productivity. The immediate effect was to give the Department a new Minister, Mrs Barbara Castle, and responsibility for incomes policy. A productivity division was promptly added to the organisation. Shortly after the creation of the enlarged Ministry, the report of the Royal Commission on Trade Unions and Employers Associations was published, bringing into active life many industrial relations questions which the Government had previously regarded as quiescent, while the Donovan Commission was considering them.

Mrs Castle's experiences as Incomes Policy overlord are discussed in detail in Chapter 4. The most important product of her term of office at the Department of Employment and Productivity seems certain to be the new legislation on industrial relations announced in a White Paper* in January 1969, and thus falling outside the period studied in this book. It can however properly be remarked that in popular estimation, as well as in the view of the Labour Party's political opponents, such action was long overdue. The period under study was characterised by growing discontent with the incidence of industrial disputes, most of them unofficial, and many of them

* *In Place of Strife*, HMSO, January 1969. Much of the projected legislation was abandoned in July, 1969, in response to TUC pressures.

causing great economic damage well beyond the companies or industries in which they occurred.

The failure of a Government otherwise strongly addicted to industrial intervention to take steps to curb this damage, must be regarded as an indication of the way in which political susceptibilities and prejudices condition the incidence of State intervention in industry.

CHAPTER THREE

Intervention via the Exchequer

Taxation is one of the oldest forms of State intervention in industry. Governments all over the world and of all political persuasions have for long used taxes on industry and on its products not just as a means of raising revenue, but as devices for discouraging or encouraging particular types of industrial or trade development.

Tariffs are, of course, the outstanding historical example. They have been applied by most countries with the deliberate and simultaneous intention of discouraging imports and enabling domestic industries to grow while protected from overseas competition. Britain's paper industry is a classical example of an industry growing to a large size while enjoying tariff protection for most of its history and then running into troubles when the protection was dismantled under EFTA. The chemical industry's growth was boosted by the Key Industries Duty imposed on imports after the 1914–18 war.

The twentieth century has seen a major extension of both the theory and practice of using the tax system as a way of implementing economic policies. Two familiar developments are the use of tax inducements to stimulate capital investment and to determine location of industry decisions.

In addition to tax measures specifically intended to influence industrial events, Governments inevitably accelerate or restrict the advance of industry by the levels of taxation they impose. A deflationary increase in taxation slows down industrial expansion, whilst reflationary measures will stimulate investment. The incidence of tax increases or decreases also has important industrial effects. In Britain the use of purchase tax, with its relatively narrow range of products, as a regulator of demand has notoriously affected the fortunes of important industries like motors and consumer durables. The impact of stop-go policies has also been disproportionately great on the capital goods and capital-intensive industries.

LABOUR'S TAX INTENTIONS

The potential which exists for use of the taxation system to influence industrial development is, of course, well known to the economic

theorists who advise politicians. Any political party, whether it has
interventionist inclinations or not, has to decide how best it can use
fiscal weapons to achieve its economic ends. Prior to the 1964
General Election Labour theorists had given a good deal of thought
to ways in which the existing tax system might be modified to stimulate economic growth. They had received a good deal of support
from non-socialist sources who wanted to see the tax system used to
stimulate capital investment and bring about more stable economic
progress. Among powerful supporters of the need for tax changes
was NEDC, which had given a good deal of attention to possible
tax changes in its study of obstacles to faster growth.* Among ideas
enjoying a fair measure of general support were the possibilities of
separating corporate and personal taxation, so that either could be
adjusted independently of the other, and for stimulating capital
investment by providing financial incentives which would be simple
to understand and would be receivable within a short time of making
the investment expenditure.

The Labour Party duly promised in its 1964 Election manifesto
a major overhaul of our tax system.† Much of the Election propaganda
concentrated on 'fairness', and the spectre of a few rich people
making huge gains and avoiding or evading tax upon them was
frequently paraded. A general capital gains tax was promised. In
more serious pronouncements on the use of the tax system to
stimulate industrial progress, Labour promised to use the tax system
to encourage industries and firms to export more and claimed that
tax policies would be used to encourage *the right type of modern
industry.* The manifesto also added—hopefully, in the light of
subsequent developments—*above all the general effect of our tax
changes will be to stimulate enterprise not to penalise it.*†

In the event, Labour's first fiscal preoccupations after taking office
were with balance of payment problems and with raising revenue
to pay for improved social welfare benefits. A fifteen per cent
'temporary' surcharge on imports was imposed although this
appeared to run counter to some of our international obligations.
Some modest assistance was given to exporters, via a rebate which
was supposed to represent a refund of indirect taxes paid on products
exported.‡ In his first Budget in November 1964 Mr Callaghan
increased duty on petrol by sixpence a gallon, and announced a rise
in the standard rate of income tax of sixpence to take effect from
April 1965. The Budget was duly hailed by Fleet Street as a 'sixpenny

* Conditions favourable to faster growth, NEDC, 1963.
† Election Manifesto, Labour Party, 1964.
‡ *The Economic Situation*, HMSO October 1964.

shocker'.* The Chancellor also announced that a capital gains tax and a corporation tax would be imposed in his next Budget.

This first Labour Budget had relatively little impact on industry, except in the respect that the promise of the imposition of corporation tax, without an indication of the rate at which it was to be levied, quite inevitably created a mood of uncertainty.

THE 1965 BUDGET

The Budget which Mr Callaghan introduced on 6 April 1965, contained several new landmarks in British fiscal practice. The Chancellor himself believed, somewhat naively, that it would ensure him a place in the history books as an enlightened tax reformer. Critics at the time disagreed strongly, and some have since been insistent that the changes Mr Callaghan introduced have been to a considerable extent responsible for the subsequent ills of the economy.

In immediate economic impact the Budget was intended to be deflationary, increasing taxation to the extent of £217 million in a full year—largely through increased tobacco, spirits, and beer duties. The main continuing impact of the Budget, however, came from Mr Callaghan's tax 'reforms', in an attack on overseas investment, and in an almost obsessive concern with tax avoidance.

The principal tax reforms were those already foreshadowed—the change to corporation tax and the introduction of a long term capital gains tax.

Mr Callaghan himself described the corporation tax as 'the most fundamental of the tax reforms' in his Budget. The essential feature was to separate the corporation from its shareholders and to impose a tax on the whole profit of the corporation, irrespective of whether it was distributed or not. Distributions were thereafter subjected to normal income tax and surtax, with no reference to the tax already paid on the profits by the corporation. The obvious intention of this change was to induce companies to retain profits by subjecting the undistributed portion to a lower effective rate of tax than had previously been the case. Conversely, distributed profits would bear much higher total taxation than before.

The introduction of corporation tax was also used to deter overseas investment by British companies by limiting the extent to which 'over-spill' relief could be set against corporation tax in respect of taxes already paid overseas. The limitation again discriminated against the shareholder, for credit for overseas tax was not to be allowed against income tax. The Chancellor recognised that this provision would cause hardship to companies with substantial

* *Daily Express*, 12 November 1964.

overseas interest and provided for two years of full transitional 'over-spill' relief which would then taper off to disappear after 1970–71. In addition, the special tax treatment of Overseas Trade Corporations was to be abolished with effect from April 1966. The justification for these changes (and for other discriminations against overseas investment introduced in the Budget) was the claim that overseas investment had in the past been treated more favourably for tax than domestic investment, but that it did not benefit the economy to the extent that investment at home did.

Apart from the effects on industry of the change to corporation tax itself, the Chancellor kept uncertainty going by confining himself to the statement that the corporation tax rate would not be over forty per cent when it was levied from April 1966 onwards. Since the corporation tax rate equivalent to the old profits and income tax rates was thirty-five per cent this left industry with the threat of a substantial increase in tax liabilities hanging over its head.

The other major change introduced was the imposition of a long term capital gains tax. The existing short term capital gains tax was extended to gains made during a period of up to twelve months, on which full income tax and surtax would be borne. The rate on long term gains was set at thirty per cent for individuals, and at the corporation tax rate for companies.

New exchange control measures were imposed to correct the alleged bias in Britain towards overseas investment. Official exchange for investment outside the sterling area was limited to projects beneficial to the balance of payments. Investors selling foreign securities were forced to exchange twenty-five per cent of the proceeds for sterling.

Among measures supposed to deter tax avoidance were abolition of all business entertainment expenditure as an allowance against tax except for entertainment of overseas buyers; the withdrawal of the initial allowance on business motor cars; and the disallowance for surtax of payments under deeds of covenant. One result of these measures was an immediate increase in business taxation of the order of at least £35 million.

REACTIONS TO THE CALLAGHAN REFORMS

Immediate reaction to Mr Callaghan's Budget was, on the whole, cautiously commendatory. The *Financial Times* described it as *good in outline, bad in parts*.* It described the level of capital gains tax as 'stiff' and commented: *a tax as heavy as this on the creation of new wealth will certainly be a considerable disincentive to the business man.* The *Economist* described the Budget as 'an accountant's nightmare'

* *Financial Times*, 7 April 1965.

and commented: *Mr Callaghan's two new landmarks in tax reform, the capital gains tax and the corporation tax, put Britain at one stroke at the top of the international league of major countries in the severity of its tax imposts on the rewards of financial investment.**

Comment became much more critical when the mammoth 226 page Finance Bill appeared and experts had the chance to consider all the implications of Mr Callaghan's 'reforms'. One factor which emerged with great clarity from the Bill was the extent to which a vast number of companies were going to be penalised under the new close company regulations. Such companies were to be forced to pay out sixty per cent of their trading income, plus the whole of their investment income as dividends (which would, of course, bear income tax and surtax). The remuneration for directors to be allowed against corporation tax was set at ridiculously low levels (for example, £11,000 for four directors).

Apart from criticism of detailed provisions of this sort, commentators began to get more and more uneasy about the overall effects of Mr Callaghan's 'reforms'. The *Economist*† suggested: *It is quite possible that, once the Bill is through, the British economy is going to be buffeted by all sorts of unintended side effects which nobody happens to have thought of yet.* It summed up its view by stating: *It is more and more apparent that Mr Callaghan's new system of business taxation is a mistake.*

It soon became apparent that the 'reforms' had been rushed into legislation without proper consideration or investigation, and that the Finance Bill itself was appallingly badly drafted. In the enormously protracted discussions of the Bill, which extended from May until August, hundreds of amendments were made, most of them coming from the Treasury itself. The most important concessions made by the Chancellor concerned the close companies and 'over-spill' relief, with extended transitional provisions applied to the latter. The *Economist* criticised the manner in which corporation tax was introduced in the following terms:‡ *The alarming conclusion that emerges from this attempt to evaluate the economic effects of the corporation tax is that this major upheaval in our tax structure has been undertaken with virtually no attempt on the part of the government to present the public with anything in the nature of a carefully argued objective and above all empirically substantiated case. It is not argued that such a case could not be made out; but the issue turns on several questions of fact which the government has not attempted to ascertain. There is, in fact, a grave suspicion that the corporation tax*

* *Economist*, 10 April 1965.
† *Economist*, 1 May 1965.
‡ *Economist*, 29 May 1965.

proposal is based on nothing more than the conjuncture of a desire to introduce a differential profits tax, the purely conceptual arguments of Mr Kaldor's minority report of the Royal Commission on Taxation, and an overwhelming desire to demonstrate the government's willingness for change. There is the danger therefore that Britain's most valuable scarce resource—its capacity for change—has been recklessly squandered.

Such were some of the responsible comments made upon Mr Callaghan's 'reforms' at the time they were being considered by Parliament. Others drew attention to the fact that the tax changes were moving Britain's system of company taxation in an entirely opposite direction to that in which major European industrial nations were adopting. Germany was taxing retained profits at a much higher rate than those distributed, while the French, only two days before Mr Callaghan presented his Budget, decided on tax changes which gave the French shareholder a much higher net yield from his investment and effectively brought the nation's tax system into line with the British system which Mr Callaghan was dismantling as *not well designed for the second half of the twentieth century.*

One immediate effect of the 1965 Finance Act was to introduce enormous additional complexity into Britain's already convoluted tax structure, and thus to place enormous demands upon the Inland Revenue and upon the accountancy profession. The Association of Certified and Corporate Accountants complained in February 1967:* *This Association has often drawn attention to the growing complexity of taxation. It is not just that the accounting and clerical processes of collecting and paying taxes are increasing in cost; much more important, tax complexities are hampering the formulation of business policy and hence the improvement of economic growth. Too much of senior executives' time is taken up on tax problems. Too much ingenuity of a high intellectual order is spent on tax avoidance which might be better applied to raising industrial efficiency. Too often the real issues involved in important business decisions are obscured by uncertainty over future tax policies, or the possible administrative interpretation of tax measures already in force. One cause of this complexity is an under-standable desire on the part of the authorities to make adjustments to the tax system which would be beneficial to the economy. However, it seems doubtful whether any recent major innovations have brought advantages to outweigh their disadvantages. At all events, they have been introduced too rapidly for the tax system to digest.* This complaint was typical of numerous others made by professional bodies about

* Association of Certified and Corporate Accountants, Memorandum to Chancellor of the Exchequer, February 1967.

the growing complexity of the tax system, to which Mr Callaghan's 'reforms' had greatly added. In Chapter 9 we consider in detail the major apparent effects of Mr Callaghan's 1965 Budget.

INVESTMENT GRANTS

The change to corporation tax was recognised to involve a reduction in the investment incentives available to industry under the old system of corporate taxation. In his Budget speech Mr Callaghan acknowledged this, but cast doubts upon the efficacy of these incentives. He promised to look into the question of a new type of investment incentive during the forthcoming year.

In January 1966, the Department of Economic Affairs published a White Paper on investment incentives, announcing a switch to a system of Investment Grants.* The grants were heavily slanted towards manufacturing investment. The rate of grant was to be twenty per cent of the actual cost of the investment, and forty per cent where the investment was made in a development area. An additional five per cent was later added for investment undertaken in 1967 and 1968.† Reduced rates of grant were payable on industrial building. The grants would be cash payments, and not offsets against taxation on profits. The payment interval would initially be eighteen months from the date of the investment, but it was hoped in due course to reduce this period to six months.

Although this scheme broadly followed what was originally suggested by NEDC, and was introduced following a good deal of investigation and consultation, considerable criticism was levelled against it. It was pointed out that the actual relief to be given to industry in respect of investment expenditure was expected to be lower than that available under the old taxation system. The bias against service industries and investment in service facilities was strongly criticised. The general principle of the scheme, that industrialists should have their investment subsidised whether or not it made profits was also queried: it was argued that the new grants would encourage investment by inefficient companies unable to earn an adequate return on their capital, leading to waste of national resources.

THE 1966 BUDGET AND SET

The Government had several bites at the budget-making cherry in 1966.

With a General Election announced for 31 March, the Chancellor, Mr Callaghan, gave a 'budget trailer' to the House of Commons on 1 March. This was primarily, of course, a political manoeuvre with

* Cmnd. 2874, and Industrial Development Act, 1966.
† S.I. 1966, No. 1569.

the Chancellor stating that he did not see the need for severe increases in taxation but would keep himself free to make any necessary changes. Mr Callaghan took advantage of the occasion to announce the switch to decimal currency proposed for February 1971, the introduction of the Government's mortgage option scheme, and new taxes on betting and gaming.

The actual Budget was presented on 3 May 1966. It included announcements that the import surcharge was to end in November, that the starting rate for corporation tax would be forty per cent, and that investment in the developed countries of the sterling area must be voluntarily reduced. There were further attacks upon what the Chancellor regarded as tax avoidance, including a provision that share options would be taxed on the difference between the price paid for shares by a director or employee and their value at the times the option was granted or taken up.

By far the most sensational feature of the Budget was yet another 'reform', the introduction from September 1966, of the Selective Employment Tax. This was in effect a payroll tax on all industry and commerce to be collected through the medium of the national insurance stamp. Manufacturing establishments would in due course receive refunds of the tax paid, plus premiums in respect of each employee. Another class of establishments, neither manufacturing nor supplying services, would receive refunds of tax paid but no premiums, while service establishments—either those actually supplying services to customers, or the offices of manufacturing companies, would pay the full tax. All companies would pay the tax, and there would be a delay in repaying refunds and premiums, so that the tax was in effect exacting a forced loan of around £250 million from industry and commerce—a loan which moreover would be kept going continuously on a revolving basis.

A number of arguments were put forward to justify the new tax. It was pointed out that the traditional concentration of indirect taxation in Britain on drink, tobacco, motoring, and goods liable to purchase tax had amounted to discrimination against manufactured goods, while services escaped without tax. Another line of justification suggested that manufacturing industries were the main providers of exports and brought more economic growth than the service industries, while the new tax was also justified on the grounds that it enabled £240 million to be taken from the economy without hitting harder traditional subjects for taxation like personal incomes and purchase tax goods.

Samuel Brittan of the *Financial Times* commented on these arguments as follows:*

* *Financial Times*, 5 May 1966.

Broadly speaking, there are two schools of thought among the supporters of the new tax. There are the enthusiasts who see it as a way of bringing about a big structural shift in the economy from services to manufacturing, and believe that this will benefit exports and growth. On the other hand, there is a more orthodox school which sees it mainly as a way of deflating the economy without having to rely once again on old faithfuls such as income-tax, purchase tax or drink and tobacco. This point of view has not had much of an airing in the initial discussion, and it deserves a little more examination. The argument that is put forward is that there is no question of discriminating against services but simply of lessening the discrimination against manufactured goods, arising from the limited coverage of the present purchase tax.

If, however, this was the Chancellor's main intention it would have been very much better if he had not given his listeners the impression that he shared the old-fashioned puritanical dislike of the service trades. Many people in the City and elsewhere, who were quite favourably disposed to the Labour Government after the recent election, now feel very bitterly that the business world is being divided on arbitrary and nonsensical principles into three sections, good, bad and indifferent. This is widely resented as a form of industrial Apartheid, which will give everyone the maximum incentive to prove that he is a true white—and not concerned with anything as iniquitous as services. (One example of the fantastic anomalies that may arise, is that there is a tax on a van driver employed by a news agency, which is supplying a service, and a subsidy on a driver employed by a newspaper which is supplying a product), and he added The Government might argue that the new tax will lead to a faster growth of manufacturing, relative to the rest of the economy than in the past, and that this will in itself increase our exports and thus provide a solution. One does not enjoy pouring cold water on a brave attempt to find a new direction in economic policy, but nevertheless this seems an enormously cumbersome and round-about route, which may not reach its intended destination.

The Selective Employment Tax has continued under attack from a very wide range of critics ever since its introduction, and the criticisms were not unnaturally massively increased when the premiums were abolished (except for development areas) immediately following devaluation, and when the levels of the tax were increased by fifty per cent with effect from September 1968.

The authorship of this tax was immediately ascribed by critics to Nicholas Kaldor, the academic economist whom Mr Callaghan had appointed as taxation adviser immediately Labour assumed office in 1964. The 1965 Budget, with its so called 'reforms' had effectively implemented Dr Kaldor's minority report to the Royal Commission on taxation in 1954. His responsibility for Selective Employment

Tax was revealingly disclosed in his inaugural lecture at Cambridge University in 1967.* This, in effect, presented the theorising behind the tax in a hypothesis that Britain's slow rate of economic growth was due to the excessive attraction of labour to the service industries and occupations. This theory has been disputed by many other economists. The effects of Selective Employment Tax are examined in Chapter 9.

THE LEVEL OF TAXATION

The Selective Employment Tax was to be the last of the Labour Government's attempts at tax reform during the period 1964–68, apart from occasional sideswipes at alleged tax avoidance practices. All Labour's future tax measures, whether imposed in the annual Budget, or in numerous mini Budgets, were to be concerned with the traditional business of removing money from the taxpayers' pocket. Mr Wilson's special measures announced on 20 July 1966, removed £500 million from the economy and clamped the £50 restriction on travel to countries outside the sterling area. A one year ten per cent surcharge was imposed on surtax. Postal service charges were raised and further restrictions were imposed on building. Hire purchase regulations were tightened. The 'voluntary' freeze on prices, incomes, and dividends was imposed.

After this massive attack on consumer and public spending, with its obvious undertones for the fortunes of British industry, the economy was to enjoy a modest respite from further deflation. Mr Callaghan's Budget in April 1967 was intended to be neutral in its effect upon the economy. A number of very minor tax changes added up to total tax remissions of £12 million. The Chancellor claimed that Labour's economic policies were working and concluded his speech with the now famous sentences: *We are now back on course. The ship is picking up speed. Every seaman knows the command at such a moment: 'Steady as she goes'.* Seven months later the pound was to be devalued!

The devaluation announcement was accompanied by a batch of tax and economic measures. Apart from a one and a half per cent rise in bank rate and £200 million cuts in public spending, corporation tax was to be increased by two and a half per cent in the next Budget, SET premiums were to be withdrawn (except in development areas) effectively increasing the tax yield by £100 million and export rebates were to be withdrawn from March 1968, increasing the effective tax burden on industry by another £100 million.

The next two months was replete with reports of agonising debates

* Kaldor N., *Causes of the Slow Rate of Economic Growth of the United Kingdom: An Inaugural Lecture* (Cambridge University Press, 1967).

within the Cabinet on cuts in public expenditure which were to be imposed to help to achieve the required shift of resources into exporting and importing saving following devaluation. On 16 January 1968 the Prime Minister announced spending cuts estimated to save £700 million. They included postponement of the projected increase in the school leaving age and the reimposition of NHS prescription charges. Measures particularly affecting industry were cuts in the road building and public housing programmes and a decision to spread payment of investment grants over a longer period.

Budget day had been fixed for 19 March and every newspaper and economic forecaster regaled the public with predictions of deflationary measures of unprecedented severity. The Chancellor (now Mr Roy Jenkins) duly obliged with tax increases estimated to increase revenue in a full year by no less than £923 million.

Purchase tax rates and customs and excise duties were substantially increased. A one year investment income levy starting at £3,000 per annum was imposed. Selective Employment Tax was increased by fifty per cent. Betting and gaming taxes were increased. Motor taxation was also increased, both by an extra fourpence per gallon tax on petrol and by an increase in road fund licences from £17 10s. to £25.

These stringent imposts, in total by far the biggest deflationary package ever imposed on the British economy, were greeted with satisfaction by most orthodox economic commentators, who agreed that the Chancellor had done enough to bring about the necessary diversion of resources into export and import saving.

It was not to be. On 22 November Mr Jenkins was on his feet again to load another £250 million of taxation on the British economy. The ten per cent regulator was applied. In addition, the Chancellor introduced the new import deposits scheme, requiring deposit of fifty per cent of the value of imported goods before customs release, with repayment to follow, without interest, after 180 days. This was to be yet another forced loan from British industry, and initial calculations suggested that it would rise to £600 million before repayments commenced. In fact, the actual burden on British industry is likely to be rather less because of help given by foreign suppliers in meeting the deposit requirements.

The addition of £2,625 million of new taxation does not tell the whole story of the Labour Government's attempts to hold down consumption and squeeze liquidity during its first four and a quarter years of office. In addition, hire purchase controls were tightened on no fewer than five occasions, while, apart from a brief period of relaxation in 1967, a progressively intensifying credit squeeze was imposed from July 1965 onwards. The process reached its climax in November 1968 when clearing banks were required to reduce total loans to the private sector by March 1969 to ninety-eight per cent of the November 1967 level. The table below shows the inexorable rise in taxation over Labour's term of office. Continuous increase of this order, coupled with an intensifying credit squeeze and other deterrents to consumption, inevitably profoundly affects industry's progress and particularly its capacity for expansion.

INCREASES IN TAXATION OCT. 1964–DEC. 1968

Date	Total additional taxation (full year £m)
Nov. 1964	215
April 1965	164
May 1966	385
July 1966	500
April 1967	–12
Nov. 1967	200
March 1968	923
Nov. 1968	250
TOTAL	2,625

Such effects are discussed in Chapter 9.

Not all the Labour Government's tax changes were made through the medium of its eight budgets and mini budgets. What was effectively a tax change of substantial significance to construction and other industries was made with the setting up of the Land Commission. Apart from receiving extensive powers of land acquisition, this body was supposed to implement Labour's promise that it would tax the profits of land speculation. It was empowered to impose a levy, initially of forty per cent, but rising in due course, on profits from increasing land values. The operations of this particular agency of intervention were the subject of considerable public disquiet in February and March 1969, when it became clear that one of its functions was to exact substantial levies on people with minimal incomes who had benefited from minor alterations in land usage. The Conservative Party has claimed that the Land Commission *merely causes land prices to rise* and is pledged to abolish it.*

* *Make Life Better*, Conservative Party, 1968.

CHAPTER FOUR

Prices and Incomes Policy

In its 1964 General Election Manifesto Labour made a good deal of its 'Plan for Stable Prices'.* In rather more muted key, it also offered a National Incomes Policy, described as *a planned growth of incomes so that they are broadly related to the annual growth of production*. The Prices and Incomes Policy thus foreshadowed has constituted a major area of intervention for the Government, and one which has proved increasingly controversial, especially among the Party's traditional allies in the Trade Union movement. There can be little doubt that what was originally envisaged was a genuinely voluntary policy. In fact, as the Government has been drawn further and further into detailed intervention on prices and incomes questions, it has found an increasing need for legal sanctions. These are due to expire during 1969, but experience to date suggests that there will be little hope of continuing to operate the policy with even moderate effectiveness unless further legal powers are taken.

The basic problem the prices and incomes policy was supposed to ameliorate was essentially that of wage inflation. Between 1958 and 1964 weekly earnings rose by 36·6 per cent; during the same period output per person employed rose by only eighteen per cent. Hourly earnings rose at a somewhat faster rate than weekly earnings owing to reductions in the working week.

During the same period total final prices rose by thirteen per cent. Retail prices rose by 15·4 per cent and export unit values by seven per cent. It will be seen that in so far as Britain had especial inflationary problems, they were much more serious in terms of wage increases outstripping productivity growth than in terms of rising prices. It was, in fact, an early criticism of Labour's prices and incomes policy that measures to influence and control prices were only introduced for political reasons—as a 'sweetener' to persuade the unions to co-operate in measures of wages restraint.

THE DECLARATION OF INTENT
Immediately following his appointment as Secretary of State for

* Labour Party Manifesto, 1964, p. 12.

Economic Affairs, Mr George Brown set out with characteristic energy and determination to secure the agreement of both sides of industry to a voluntary prices and incomes policy. By early December the newspapers were reporting that agreement was in sight and on 16 December the 'Joint Statement of Intent on Productivity, Prices and Incomes' was signed by representatives of the Trades Union Congress, the Federation of British Industries, the British Employers' Federation, the National Association of British Manufacturers and the Association of British Chambers of Commerce. Among the various rolling phrases with which the document is replete the following probably represent the key to what was intended:

> to ensure that British industry is dynamic and that its prices are competitive;
> to raise productivity and efficiency so that real national output can increase, and to keep increases in wages, salaries and other forms of incomes in line with this increase;
> to keep the general level of prices stable.

Mr George Brown described it as *a truly historic achievement, which puts Britain in the first rank of countries seeking solutions to the basic problems of industrial society.* Most commentators did not rank the statement quite so highly and concentrated on pointing out the almost innumerable problems of principle and practice which would have to be overcome before the Declaration could be translated into meaningful action. The signatories to the document too had more reservations, and more appreciation of the practical difficulties ahead, than the bold wording of the Declaration made clear.

Somewhat to the discomfiture of those involved, Mr George Brown and his aides immediately began to behave as though all trade unionists and all industrialists had been whole-heartedly committed by the Declaration. A number of trade association chiefs and company bosses were summoned to the DEA and invited to explain decisions they had taken to increase prices. Some industrialists and retail chains, including Sainsbury's and Marks and Spencer's, voluntarily pledged co-operation to try to keep prices stable, with some consequential publicity benefits.

The Department's officials held detailed discussions with the management organisations and the TUC to hammer out machinery for working the policy and consultations were held with NEDC to help determine the official criteria against which price rises and wage increases were to be judged. The measures agreed were set out in a White Paper 'Machinery of Prices and Incomes Policy'.*

* Cmnd 2577.

The main element in the machinery was to be the setting up of a National Board for Prices and Incomes. The Board was set up under the Chairmanship of Mr Aubrey Jones, in April 1965, and the first three references were made to it by the Government on 6 May. These were all price references, covering standard bread and flour, soap and detergents and road haulage rates. The first wage reference, concerning the printing industry, was made on 18 May, but costs and prices were also included. The Board published its first report—on road haulage rates—on 28 June 1965.*

The Board condemned the Road Haulage Association's practice of recommending blanket price increases to its members. The following day the Association agreed to make no general recommendation for future increases in charges, but insisted that its members would be justified in making an immediate increase in haulage rates.

The publication of the report, and the Road Haulage Association's reactions to it, produced the first of several *causes célèbres* in which Mr George Brown was involved on the Prices and Incomes Policy. Others were to follow at irregular intervals throughout his period of office in the Department of Economic Affairs. His technique was to summon leaders of an industry once a Prices and Incomes Board report had appeared and to invite them to operate the Board's proposals. Refusal to agree put the full blast of publicity on to the heads of the unfortunate industrialists concerned, often giving the public impression that the industry was unjustifiably increasing its prices in face of heroic efforts by the Government to protect the consumer.

As 1965 progressed it became clear that the Prices and Incomes Policy could hardly function effectively if the National Board for Prices and Incomes was required to adjudicate on price or wage increases which had already occurred. Consideration was accordingly given to ideas for setting up an 'early warning' system. These proposals were accepted in September by the Confederation of British Industry and the Trades Union Congress. On 11 November 1965, a White Paper† was published outlining arrangements for voluntary notification of intended price increases and claims and settlements relating to pay.

By the end of 1965 the National Board for Prices and Incomes had published seven reports. The five concerned with prices had mostly been successful to at least the extent of holding back some price increases which might otherwise have occurred. The two wage references had little discernible effect on the course of wages. With the early warning system getting underway, it could reasonably be

* Cmnd 2695.
† Cmnd 2808.

claimed that the Policy had got off to a promising start. There was however, one cloud on the horizon. Britain's biggest trade union, the Transport and General Workers' Union, had decided against the policy and thus begun an opposition which was to last throughout the period under study.

The year 1966 began with one of those flurries over prices which were characteristic of Mr Brown's years of office at the DEA. On 10 January Ranks Hovis McDougall announced increases in bread prices while awaiting an interim report from the National Board for Prices and Incomes. The Minister at once attacked this action, although nine days later the PIB Report* was to approve the announced price increases.

In February the first of a long series of Prices and Incomes Bills providing legal penalties for violations was published. Following the Election, the Bill had to be reintroduced and on 4 July a revised and somewhat tougher version was published.† It effectively marked the end of the voluntary Prices and Incomes Policy. On the day prior to its publication, Mr Frank Cousins, General Secretary of the Transport and General Workers' Union, showed his disagreement with the change in policy by resigning his Cabinet appointment as Minister of Technology.

On 20 July the Prime Minister announced his 1966 package of deflationary measures. They included a 'voluntary' freeze on prices and wages. On 9 August Mr George Brown was moved to the Foreign Office from the Department of Economic Affairs, after prolonged consideration of the possibility of resigning from the Government altogether. His grievances lay in the general conduct of economic policy and the implicit abandonment of the National Plan rather than in the new forms of incomes policy.

The Prices and Incomes Act gave the Government reserve powers of legal compulsion to order the provision of information to the Prices and Incomes Board, and to make orders deferring wage or price increases. Government spokesmen had proclaimed that these powers might well never have to be used, but by 4 October the compulsory provisions (part IV of the Act) had been activated and by 14 October the new Minister for Economic Affairs—now Mr Michael Stewart—had made compulsory orders to Thorn Electrical Industries and the Newspaper Proprietors' Association halting increases in wages.

These Orders were the signal that the Government was prepared to operate the freeze with full rigour. As interpreted by the new Minister, however, there were extraordinary anomalies. Increases due to

* Cmnd 2878.
† HC Bill, 1966–67, No. 70.

D

employees working on fixed salary scales were permitted, while they were forbidden for those where salary increases were normally given at the employer's discretion. The effect of this extraordinary ruling was that Government and local authority employees duly got their rises during the freeze, while executives in private industry were denied them. Similarly, increases due under a number of productivity agreements were quite irrationally forbidden during the period.

The first half of 1967 saw the ending of the freeze, which was superseded by the so-called period of severe restraint. The norm for incomes increases was still nil, but there were a number of conditions under which wage increases could in fact be allowed. Most of these were aimed at rewarding increases in productivity, but there were also special provisions for the lower paid.*

It had for long been clear that the work of the statutory Wages Councils took little regard for the Prices and Incomes Policy criteria. These Councils had historically looked after the interests of workers in industries where trade union representation was weak. Their traditional function was to try to ensure that the wages of people in the industries they covered kept up with the cost of living and were broadly comparable with those paid in the other industries. Since most of the reports on wages prepared by the National Board for Prices and Incomes had gone out of their way to attack comparability and rises in the cost of living as criteria for wage increases, it was clear that there was considerable incompatibility between the approach of the Board and that of the Wages Councils.

The issue came to a head on 9 March 1967, when the Board Report No. 27 'Pay of workers in the Retail Drapery, Outfitting, and Footware Trades'† was published. It criticised the approach of the Wages Councils, particularly their attitudes to comparability and the cost of living and recommended reductions in their recent awards.

The Retail Wages Council at once rejected the Board's report. The eventual solution was that most of the Wage Council awards were approved by the Minister of Labour, though he accompanied this approval with a recommendation that the Wages Councils' awards should only be paid to workers on minimum rates.

On 21 March the latest in the series of White Papers on Prices and Incomes Policy was published.‡ It proposed a *year of moderation* in prices and wage increases after the period of severe restraint ended on 30 June. A voluntary 'vetting' system to be run by the TUC and the CBI was supposed to replace compulsory notification.

The CBI in fact found it both impracticable and undesirable to

* Cmnd 3150.
† Cmnd 3224.
‡ Cmnd 3235.

attempt to run a price vetting system. The Trade Union Congress went ahead with the development of its own system for scrutinising and advising upon applications for wage increases, forming a voluntary screening system which is credited with securing the abandonment or modification of many wage proposals which were widely at odds with the Incomes Policy. In total, however, no really effective voluntary system was achieved and the Government took further powers of compulsion to delay price and wage increases for up to seven months.* Its resolve was doubtless strengthened in September by the publication of an IMF Report urging the operation of a tight Incomes Policy to strengthen international competitiveness.

The next major event in the progress of Incomes Policy was perhaps the succession of Lord Carron as President of the Amalgamated Engineering Federation by the Left wing Mr Hugh Scanlon. This change brought Britain's second biggest trade union into opposition to Incomes Policy, or at least to its compulsory provisions.

Before the month of November was out Britain had devalued and the Prices and Incomes Board had been asked to investigate a variety of post-devaluation price increases, most of which were subsequently found to be justifiable.

The over-riding aim of economic policy during 1968 was to hold back domestic consumption so as to permit a shift of resources into investment, import saving, and exporting. On 5 January the Prime Minister told the TUC that pay rises for the year commencing in July 1968 must be held to a three and a half per cent maximum. After a period of consultations and behind the scenes arguments, a White Paper was published on 3 April announcing legislation permitting the Government to freeze wages for twelve months pending Reports by the Prices and Incomes Board, to order price reductions, and to control rents and dividends.† Three days later Mrs Barbara Castle became Secretary of State for Employment and Productivity (the old Ministry of Labour) and assumed responsibilities for wages policy. One of her early actions was to freeze for three months a one pound per week rise for municipal busmen as incompatible with Incomes Policy. The Agreement had already undergone a four months suspension pending an NBPI Report, and the DEP were to freeze the increase for a further five months on 10 July, making twelve months of suspension in all.

One of the more sensational developments in Incomes Policy was a threat by the DEP to refer to the Prices and Incomes Board a £4,500 rise in the salary of the Chairman of Hambros Bank, who had recently gone on record criticising the Prime Minister as the worst

* HC Paper, 1966–67, No. 227.
† Cmnd 3590.

since Lord North. In the event, the reference announced on 1 July covered the salaries of chairmen and board members of private and nationalised industries generally.

The second half of 1968 was largely marked by increasing readiness to use the compulsory powers to freeze wage increases pending or following NBPI Reports. Among groups affected were wages in the building industry and those of two large groups of ICI employees. On the other hand, critics of the Policy hastened to point out that large groups of employees who could do major damage to the economy by strike action had been apparently treated with much greater leniency. Such criticism particularly related to settlements on the railways and in the engineering industry, directly promoted by the DEP and, in the opinion of many observers, driving a coach and horses through the Policy.

This brief and factual summary of the progress of Prices and Incomes Policy over its four years of operation does not, perhaps, do justice to the passions and controversies it has aroused.

The Policy was quite inevitably controversial right from its inception. It was undoubtedly only initially accepted by industrialists and the trade unions as a result of Mr George Brown's assurances back in the heady days of December 1964, that the whole process was to be voluntary. Even with such assurances many of those who originally promised co-operation did so with a great many reservations. The addition of increasing compulsory elements quite naturally led many who would give qualified support to a genuinely voluntary system into either the most reluctant acquiescence or tacit or outright opposition. Whatever the qualifications and the disclaimers that compulsory powers were to be only temporary, it was clear that they effectively amounted to an apparatus for State control of prices and wages. Apart from the implication of such powers for individual liberties it was quite reasonable for industrialists to doubt whether compulsory price controls could be compatible with economic efficiency, especially when emphasis in Prices Policy was concentrated on politically sensitive commodities like bread and beer.

Much more complex problems faced trade union leaders. A distrust of State control over wages was a natural and instinctive reaction for them and for their more militant members. One problem for trade union leaders, however moderate, was how far they could co-operate in an Incomes Policy, particularly how far they could acquiesce in compulsory controls without surrendering effective union leadership to the more militant members of their organisations. An equally critical problem lay in the extent to which the various approvals and disapprovals granted to wage increases by the Prices and Incomes Board and responsible Ministers appeared to be fair. A

tendency by the Government to retreat from Incomes Policy criteria
when major industrial disputes were threatened, but to preserve the
rigour of the Policy in wage issues where little worker disruptive power
was involved, was a major factor in the disquiet of union leaders
about Incomes Policy. Such factors have been among the principal
causes of growing trade union hostility to the operation of a
compulsory Incomes Policy—fully expressed by such things as the
1968 TUC Congress vote 7·7 million to 1 million for the repeal of
the 1968 Prices and Incomes Act.

Union opposition and criticisms from its own party Left wing
have left a good deal of doubt on whether it will be politically possible
for the Government to assume yet another batch of compulsory
powers, however allegedly 'temporary', when the present ones
expire at the end of the year. In March 1969, David Watt, Political
Editor of the *Financial Times*, in an article on the forthcoming
Budget, commented: *Two years ago it might have been possible to
avoid the worst consequences of this dilemma by combining expansion
with a compulsory Prices and Incomes policy, and indeed this is what
Mr George Brown and Lord Balogh are still rather forlornly advocating.
But, alas, this way out is now firmly blocked. Prices and Incomes
Policy is dead already and will be buried by Christmas. It is not Mr
Jenkins' fault that this card was played to take the wrong trick—the
defence of the old exchange rate—but I have been able to find no one
either in the Cabinet or outside it who seriously believes that it is worth
anything today.**

In the absence of compulsory powers there seems little doubt that
the Policy would be almost wholly ineffective—at least in containing
the growth of incomes—so that 1969 may well see the end (whether
acknowledged or not) of the experiment on which Labour embarked
so hopefully in its first days of power.

* *Financial Times*, 28 March 1969.

CHAPTER FIVE

Intervention via regional development

Attempts to ameliorate hardship caused by regions of high unemployment constitute one of the longest-established forms of Government intervention. In Britain they date back to the Special Areas Act of 1934. They are parallelled by measures over a similar period introduced by the governments of many other industrial nations.

The problems of regional 'imbalance' constitute the growing pains of industrial economies. In mature industrial nations like Britain, France and the United States, the main and obvious manifestation is the development of areas of heavy and persistent unemployment as once-dominant industries decline or change their location. The problem reached major proportions in Britain during the inter-war years when successive depressions led to increasing hardship in industries such as coal-mining, ship-building, heavy engineering and textiles. The result was disproportionately high unemployment in areas such as Scotland, the North-east and South Wales. The problems caused by the decline of older industries tend to be accentuated by the reluctance on the part of new and growing industry to move into the older industrial regions. This is in part due to the fact that past developments have made these areas physically unattractive and often provided with an infrastructure which is outdated. It is also due to the fact that for many of the newer industries former location factors such as proximity to coal supplies, ports and particular climates are much less important than access to the growing markets and industrial services of the Midlands and South-east. Through the working of these factors some regions of Britain have been faced with both a decline in existing employment opportunities and a much lower than average rate of provision of new employment opportunities.

This is the basic regional problem of the mature industrial nations. In countries where industrialisation is a more recent development, the typical problem is that certain regions become the focus for rapid industrialisation and advance in prosperity and employment opportunities at a much faster rate than regions which fail to attract industry. There are thus major regional disparities with massive inter-regional migration. The best known example in Europe of this process is in Italy where industrial expansion has proceeded at a very rapid pace in the North, while in the South (the Mezzo-giorno) low-level standards have persisted and there has been a massive exodus of population seeking industrial work in the Milan and Turin areas.

In the mature industrial countries and particularly in Britain, this regional imbalance has produced some concomitant problems. The most obvious has been the growth of congestion in the South-east and Midland areas. Alongside this has been the problem of regional 'over-heating'. During boom periods in Britain the prosperous regions have been the first to experience excessive unfilled vacancies and substantial wages drift as companies have sought to attract labour. Difficulties in these regions have prompted successive administrations to apply 'stops' to the whole national economy at times when there has still been considerable unemployment in the less prosperous regions.

This situation has prompted economists and politicians to form a variety of theories about under-used resources and regional balance. The existence of pools of unemployed in certain regions has in-evitably suggested that faster economic growth would be possible if some means could be found for bringing the unemployed into productive work. The function of high-prosperity regions in acting as inflationary pace-makers has led to theories that holding back industrial development in these regions and concentrating it upon the less prosperous regions would enable both to proceed without inflation.

Naturally enough, disparities in regional prosperity have presented considerable political problems in democratic nations. The people who live in the less prosperous regions are voters, often with in aggregate a decisive influence on which party gains or retains power. The current development areas in Britain, for example, contain forty per cent of the electorate. Inevitably votes are more likely to be given to those politicians who offer measures likely to ameliorate regional unemployment than to those who appear to be ignoring the problem. This inevitably constrains parties in power to achieve some kind of impact on the problems of regional imbalance, while those in opposition tend to outbid them by advising further measures or more radical solutions. These political constraints are powerful generators of interventionist policies.

PRE-1964 MEASURES

The traditional means by which Governments attempt to ameliorate regional unemployment are the offering of inducements to industrialists to set up new enterprises in these regions. Following from the 1934 Act, companies contemplating a move to the Special Areas, or expansion within them, could hope for a new factory to rent, the financing of part of their capital needs and some subsidy towards overhead costs and profits. These features have persisted in Britain ever since and have been progressively made more generous. They have, incidentally, been introduced or imitated in many other European countries.

The next stage in the evolution of regional development policies was the taking of powers to prohibit industrial development in areas deemed undesirable by the authorities, with the obvious and intended consequence of forcing companies either to shift their development plans to some other area or to forgo them altogether. The post-war Labour Government inherited very strong powers to direct industry as part of the war-time controls. It also had a great deal of vacant factory space left by munitions and other war-time industries which it could offer on advantageous terms to those willing to move into the less prosperous regions. Powers of permanent control were taken under the Town and Country Planning Act of 1947. This, among other things, introduced Industrial Development Certificates which have persisted to the present day. The Act required that any planning application for manufacturing premises of over 5,000 sq. ft. in area must be accompanied by an Industrial Development Certificate issued by the Board of Trade, affirming that the proposed development was in accordance with *the proper distribution of industry*.

The use of Industrial Development Certificates to force companies into the less prosperous areas has varied greatly in rigour over the years. During the early fifties Certificates were issued with relatively little restriction, except in the most congested areas of the Southeast and Midlands. From 1958 onwards the Board of Trade substantially modified this policy. To quote one commentator:* *it now began to refuse IDCs everywhere except in the Development Areas, despite continuing protests from moderately prosperous localities that they could accommodate new industry without adding to their own traffic or housing problems, and also protests from some overspill reception areas that applications for development there which would previously have been granted were now being refused, and that the Board of Trade was thus impeding the policy of the Ministry of Housing and Local Government.* In the same year new legislation was introduced empowering the Treasury to make grants or loans to undertakings likely to reduce unemployment in the Development Areas. The legislation also added a number of new localities to the areas entitled to receive Government assistance to reduce unemployment.

The policy of attempting to attract new industry to the less prosperous regions through Government financial assistance and the

* B. J. Loasby, *District Bank Review,* December 1965.

provision of premises was continued and extended by the Conservative administration during the 1960s. The Local Employment Act of 1960 codified and extended the existing provisions, while the Act of 1963 made the benefits available as a matter of right rather than at the discretion of the Board of Trade or the Industrial Estates Management Corporations. At the same time 'free depreciation' was granted to all industrial firms in Development Districts, constituting a further substantial addition to the armoury of financial attractions. Among other measures undertaken by the Conservative Administrations, was considerable behind-the-scenes pressure on major industrialists to locate new expansion projects in the Development Districts. Among the obvious fruits of this pressure was the setting up of plants on Merseyside, in Scotland and in South Wales by the big motor manufacturers.

CHANGES SINCE 1964

As we have seen, Labour inherited a system of measures which provided two forms of inducement to industrialists to move or to expand in the Development Areas. One set of inducements consisted of the provision of factories, with grants or loans towards the cost of setting up or expanding. The second set of inducements were substantial tax off-sets for industrialists in these regions, particularly 'free depreciation'. The Industrial Development Certificate system, which Labour itself had introduced in 1947, was also inherited intact and with a recent tradition of relatively tough application to force as much new industrial activity as possible to the Development Districts. The Conservatives had also started some rudimentary forms of regional planning.

Faithful, in this particular case, to its election pledges the Labour Government has made extremely extensive additions to this inheritance. The Development Districts themselves have been massively extended so that they now cover over fifty per cent of the total area of the country. The financial inducements have been substantially augmented, with two kinds of wage subsidy now provided for industry in the Development Areas. Restrictions on expansion in the non-Development Areas have been harshly increased, with the exemption limits for Industrial Development Certificates substantially lowered and major restrictions on office building introduced. Building licensing was also introduced by Labour in 1964 but relaxed in 1968. Training facilities in the Development Areas have been substantially increased and grants to facilitate re-training have been provided. In addition to all this an elaborate network of regional planning activities has been launched under co-ordination by the Department of Economic Affairs.

NEW INDUCEMENTS

A substantial amount of ingenuity has been devoted to augmenting and extending inducements to companies to move to or expand in the Development Areas. The traditional forms of financial help given by the Board of Trade have been continued with a steady rise in their total value from £10 million in 1964 to £23 million in 1968. A major change in the provision of capital inducements was effected by the substitution of investment grants for allowances to be set against profits in 1966. These grants, payable whether or not profits are earned, gave a substantial premium to Development Area capital investment. The rate of grants for manufacturing equipment was initially set at forty per cent in the Development Areas, against twenty per cent in other areas. These rates were increased to forty-five per cent and twenty-five per cent respectively for investment under-taken and paid for during the years 1967 and 1968. Unlike the former initial allowances and 'free depreciation' these grants exclude service industry investment and investment in buildings. These exclusions, plus the abolition of 'free depreciation', have the basic effect of making the capital assistance given little, if any, more generous than that previously available to the average company. On balance, manufacturing industries thinking of moving to the Development Areas, or expanding therein, may be slightly better off, but to service industries the capital inducements are less attractive than under the former system.

The quite novel forms of inducement introduced by Labour are two forms of wage subsidy. When Selective Employment Tax was introduced in 1966, it was provided that, within the relatively crude definitions of the scheme, a premium should be paid on refunds of the tax for manufacturing employees in all regions. This arrangement was changed without prior notice at the time of devaluation in November 1967 and the premium was thereafter only payable in respect of manufacturing employees in the Development Areas. The premium is worth 7s 6d per week per employee to manufacturing companies in these areas.

The second form of wage premium, the Regional Employment Premium (REP), was mooted in a Green Paper in 1967.* The scheme was to pay a weekly premium to employers in respect of all employees in manufacturing industry in the Development Areas. A number of claims were made in respect of this idea. One of the basic attractions was that it would help to attract labour intensive employment to the regions, as distinct from the capital intensive operations which concentration on investment subsidies had tended to encourage. It was argued that the boost to profitability which the premium would

* Cmnd 3310.

give to companies in the Development Areas would, in due course, lead to increases in taxable capacity and thus make the cost of the premium self-liquidating. It was dogmatically claimed that the premium would not find its way into wage levels and cause wage inflation.

The Green Paper was issued as a basis for discussion and not as a statement of Government policy. Despite this ostensible open-mindedness, the Government brushed aside some fairly powerful critics in deciding to proceed with the idea. A major critic was the Confederation of British Industry, which had a number of reservations about the scheme and especially doubted claims that the premium would not find its way into wage levels.* It also drew attention to the anomalies which would arise in relative wage costs between companies which happen to be on different sides of arbitrarily drawn boundaries between Development Areas and other areas. Payment of the Regional Employment Premium began in April 1968 and the current cost is £96 million per year.†

The latest chapter in the evolution of regional policy was the creation of 'special development areas' in 1967. The background was alarm at the prospects of soaring unemployment in Scotland, the North-east and Wales as a result of the colliery closures envisaged by the National Coal Board. The Board was asked to slow the closure programme and the special development areas were instituted. The Department of Economic Affairs summarised the new scheme as follows:‡

Further assistance is now being made available to a limited number of areas within the Development Areas which may suffer from exceptionally high unemployment through colliery closures. The incentives which will be available to new projects providing suitable employment include a rent-free period of up to five years for firms renting Board of Trade factories; thirty-five per cent building grants, and loans at moderate rates of interest towards the balance of building costs; and new grants towards operating costs.

In Chapter 11 we study the apparent effects of regional policies, and particularly of the Labour Government's additions, to try to ascertain how far they have achieved their local aims and what their effects have been on the economy as a whole.

* CBI Regional Study, September 1968.
† Parliamentary Answer, *Hansard*, 4 March 1969.
‡ DEA progress report No. 35, December 1967.

CHAPTER SIX

New agencies of intervention

One of the criticisms to which interventionist politicians are subject is the charge that they are interfering in matters in which they have insufficient knowledge and experience. Thus in the wave of nationalisation which occurred during Mr Attlee's administrations the Government was careful to entrust the management of the newly nationalised industries to boards or corporations theoretically composed of expert managers and free from day to day political interference.

Once intervention moves away from the well-worn track of outright nationalisation ministers once more lay themselves open to charges of interference on the basis of inadequate knowledge. Moreover, it is difficult for ministers to give the essential impression of being 'fair' in their decisions on industrial matters. Not only are their political opponents likely to see inequity in what they decide, but the variety of vested interests are equally likely to feel hard done by.

Mr Wilson's Government has shown considerable ingenuity in avoiding these pitfalls by the creation of new agencies which could play a highly interventionist role without incurring criticisms of political or other bias or charges of inexpertise.

THE NATIONAL BOARD FOR PRICES AND INCOMES

The first of these new creations was the National Board for Prices and Incomes. Since it followed directly from the signing of the 'Declaration of Intent' in December 1964 it could be claimed that this particular body was set up with the approval of both sides of industry. The Board was preliminarily constituted in March 1965 with Royal Commission status. In 1966, when incomes policy was given legal sanctions (and the Board itself was given powers to compel the disclosure of information) it was converted to a statutory board. Mr Aubrey Jones, the former Conservative Minister of Supply, was appointed the Board's chairman on its formation for a five year term. Throughout its history to date, the Board has consisted of around thirteen members; membership has always included a sprinkling of industrialists and trade unionists, but the general bias in personnel has been towards academic economists.

The basic function of the Prices and Incomes Board has been essentially judicial. Its main task has been to examine incomes, prices, and productivity questions referred to it by the Government, and to decide whether the proposed course of action (usually a wage or price increase) conformed with whatever prices and incomes policy 'criteria' happened to be in force at the time. The Board's findings have had no legal authority. During the voluntary phase of Prices and Incomes Policy it was up to the parties concerned to accept or reject the Board's recommendations as they saw fit—and subject to whatever pressures the Minister concerned could apply. Since Prices and Incomes policy has acquired compulsory elements it has been up to the Government department concerned to accept or reject the recommendations of the Board and give them effect in legally binding Orders.

Although the Prices and Incomes Board has thus been confined to a basic judicial role even its harshest critics can hardly accuse it of failing to exercise its functions in a constructive manner. What the Board has generally sought to do is to provide specific recommendations on how inflationary price or wage increases can be avoided through the attainment of higher efficiency. Many such recommendations have been unexceptionable and, indeed, statements of the obvious. From time to time (and understandably, perhaps, in view of the fact that the Board is always under pressure to produce its reports quickly) its recommendations have been subjected to substantial criticisms on the basis of superficiality or failing to obtain all the essential information.

Full details of the work of the Board exist in three General Reports it has published to date.* These reports also give some interesting indications on the Board's own views (or at least those of its chairman) on the limitations under which it has been required to operate and of the functions which it believes it could fulfil. The main limitations lie in the fact that the Board can only deal with matters specifically referred to it by Government Departments, and by the constraints imposed through having to work within criteria which the Board has not itself devised.

The effect of these limitations has been to give the Prices and Incomes Board a relatively marginal role in the wage negotiating scene. One derisive critic† has indeed characterised the Chairman of the Board as *a persistent, if largely ineffective, advocate of productivity agreements on the outer fringe of wage bargaining*. The Board's influence has also been reduced by the relative triviality of many of the references made to it, by the failure of Ministers and the parties

* 1966—Cmnd 3087; 1967—Cmnd 3394; 1968—Cmnd 3715.
† Auberon Waugh, *Spectator*, 11 April 1969.

concerned to act on many of its recommendations, and above all by the unwillingness of the Government to refer major pay claims to the Prices and Incomes Board when they involve groups of workers likely to damage the economy through industrial action if their demands were not met.

The effectiveness of the National Board for Prices and Incomes is clearly bound up with that of the policy which it exists to interpret. We examine the apparent effects of Prices and Incomes Policy in Chapter 10 and conclude that there is little prospect or reason for its continuing survival, at least in its present compulsory and detailed form. This would logically suggest the disappearance of the Board, though there might be possible advantages in its survival as a kind of occasional advisory body on Prices and Incomes questions of crucial importance to the economy.

THE INDUSTRIAL REORGANISATION CORPORATION

In January 1966 the press began to buzz with rumours of plans thought up by the backroom boys of the Department of Economic Affairs to set up a new Government agency based on the State Holding Company concept embodied in Italy's IRI (Institute for Industrial Reorganisation). These rumours were duly confirmed with the publication of a White Paper* outlining the scheme and proposing an initial £150 million of Government money to be put at the disposal of the Agency. Industry greeted the idea with instant hostility, and the Board of Imperial Chemical Industries in due course took the unprecedented step of publishing a statement condemning the proposed Corporation. None of this hostility caused the Government to modify its proposals and before long announcements were made that Sir Frank Kearton, then Managing Director of Courtaulds, was to be the Corporation's chairman and Mr Ronald Grierson, a merchant banker, was to be Managing Director. A number of industrialists, some of them of considerable eminence, and some trade unionists accepted invitations to join the Board of 'the Corporation. Labour was able to claim during its 1966 General Election campaign, that the new Corporation would reconstruct British industry to everyone's advantage.

In fact, there was a long period of quiescence during which the Board was criticised by Labour zealots for apparently doing nothing. Its first announced actions were not an especially happy augury, since they involved it in taking a holding in the Rootes Group to prevent its total dominance by American interests as a result of the Chrysler take-over. This was to be the first of a number of occasions on which the IRC was to act in what can only be described as the spirit of

* Cmnd 2889.

industrial nationalism. Thereafter the Corporation settled down to pursue what has in general been a pacific and constructive role in promoting voluntary mergers, punctuated every now and then by its involvement in support of one side or the other in take-over contests.

Details of the various routine and uncontroversial matters in which the Corporation has been involved are contained in the Annual Reports published by the Corporation. There are perhaps two comments which might reasonably be made on this and particular aspects of the Corporation's work. Many of the developments which occur under the influence of the Corporation could apparently equally well have been achieved without its intervention through normal commercial agencies such as merchant banks, or on the initiative of the parties concerned. Where this has not been the case, it has generally been the role of the Corporation to provide finance which would presumably not have been forthcoming on commercial terms. Such was the case in the British Leyland merger, and in the merger between English Electric and Elliott Automation. The suspicion in such cases —and especially in the financial assistance given to British paper companies to set up de-inking plants—is that the Corporation's role has been largely confined to providing 'soft' finance to companies who did not really need such assistance, or for projects which were of such dubious value in the eyes of the capital market that they did not rate support.

The more controversial operations of the Industrial Reorganisation Corporation are inevitably those where it has engaged in discrimination against particular companies and used its State-provided funds to ensure the outcome which it desired. The first overt example of such discrimination came in November 1966 when the Corporation let it be known that it supported the contested General Electric Company bid for Associated Electrical Industries. This discrimination led directly to the resignation of Sir Charles Wheeler from the Board of the Industrial Reorganisation Corporation, and it was soon followed by the resignation of Mr Ronald Grierson (who was replaced as Managing Director by another merchant banker, Mr Charles Villiers).

A few months later the Industrial Reorganisation Corporation was engaged in its most notorious discriminatory operation during the period under study, when it actively prevented the Rank Organisation from acquiring Cambridge Instruments, and instead promoted and financed a merger between Cambridge and George Kent Limited. Features of this episode which aroused great controversy were the Corporation's use of Government funds to buy Cambridge shares in the market and directly from the Royal Society, and the fact that this action deprived other Cambridge shareholders of the chance to accept a slightly higher bid for their shares from Rank. It was also pointed out that the Industrial Reorganisation Corporation had made possible for George Kent a take-over operation which was far beyond the financial resources it could have deployed itself. The justification which the IRC claimed for this very clear-cut piece of discrimination was 'industrial logic'. It argued that the Rank take-over of Cambridge, which would have resulted in the formation of a very large Rank subsidiary devoted wholly to scientific instruments, was less 'in the national interest' than the Kent/Cambridge merger which created a group covering both industrial and scientific instruments. Such arguments are by their nature inconclusive—as the IRC's own former Managing Director, Mr Ronald Grierson, has pointed out:* *there is no yardstick by which the fashionable concept of 'industrial logic' can be assessed. The term is used as if it had an objective meaning whereas it is of course totally subjective. What is logical to some is quite illogical to others. One has only to listen to the views of different industrialists in the same sector of industry to appreciate that there is more than a single solution to any one problem.*

The essence of the IRC's discrimination in favour of GEC and George Kent (and later supporting the GEC merger with English Electric in opposition to the proposed take-over of English Electric by Plessey) was that it broke the IRC's tradition of assisting with restructuring projects among willing partners and moved the Corporation into an active and discriminatory interventionist role. Its part in the Kent/Cambridge affair was widely condemned by industry, and the Confederation of British Industry pointed out that the Corporation had forfeited much of the confidence which since its foundation it had slowly and painfully built up among industrialists.

Critics at the time pointed out a characteristic of the IRC's conception which most industrialists regard as highly objectionable and dangerous. In the words of the *Spectator*,† the Corporation is *in the precise sense of the word, irresponsible.* Put another way, industrialists' objections centred very strongly on the fact that there are no formal limits upon what the Corporation may do except that it has no powers of compulsion. Within this proviso it has apparently unlimited powers to interfere and to pursue or promote any course of action it deems desirable. There were powerful calls in Parliament, following the Cambridge Instrument affair, for restriction of the IRC's terms of reference, but these were refused by Government spokesmen.

When the formation of the IRC was first announced, many critics expressed the fear that it would in practice prove an instrument of backdoor nationalisation. Such criticisms were dismissed at the time

---

* *Sunday Telegraph*, 2 March 1969.
† Christopher Fildes, *Spectator*, 21 June 1968.

by Government spokesmen and little in effect happened during the period under study which can be said to justify them. Some confirmation of the claims of critics was, however, forthcoming in February 1969 when the IRC itself took over the firm of Brown Bayley with the aim of merging its ball-bearing interests with those of other British manufacturers and selling off its steel making interests to the British Steel Corporation.

Apart from these 'creeping nationalisation' implications, this action had other overtones which many people found disquieting. The objection was that the IRC's moves in the ball-bearing industry were primarily designed to prevent further expansion in this country to the big Swedish group SKF. This was a manifestation of industrial nationalism which is hardly likely to be of ultimate benefit to Britain in an era when trans-national companies are likely to dominate the world scene and the nation has a vital interest in participating in as many of such groups as possible. It is also, it need hardly be emphasised, a philosophy which invites retaliation.

The controversy surrounding the IRC indicates fairly clearly the rather dubious role it was set up to fulfil and the extent to which it has been given a free hand to act in ways which many of its critics regard as arbitrary. It seems likely that the return of a Conservative administration would either see the abolition of the IRC or a drastic reduction in its freedom of action.

INCREASED WORK FOR THE MONOPOLIES COMMISSION

The Labour Government has used the Monopolies Commission much more actively than its predecessors. One of its early pieces of legislation was the 1965 Monopolies and Mergers Act which gave the Government powers to require the publication of regulated prices and to order the dissolution of monopolies. The Act also gave new powers to refer to the Monopolies Commission mergers meeting certain tests of size (either market share or absolute size) and gave the Board of Trade powers to suspend proposed mergers pending enquiry by the Commission, and to forbid their implementation following the Commission's report.

The provisions on proposed mergers were in fact similar to those which exist in many other countries, notably those operated under anti-trust legislation in America. During our period under study they were not used to any great extent, though certain mergers such as those proposed between United Drapery and Montague Burton, and between the Ross Group and Associated Fisheries were forbidden. In 1969 the powers were invoked on a rather wider basis when two conglomerate-type mergers were referred to the Commission.

E

The existence of a body to promote mergers (the IRC) simultaneously with powers to prevent mergers obviously gave scope for a good deal of discriminatory intervention in industry, and it also foreshadowed the appearance of some apparent contradictions and anomalies, since mergers promoted by the IRC were exempt from reference to the Monopolies Commission. The anomalies duly appeared. For example, the Ross Group/Associated Fisheries merger which the Monopolies Commission had disallowed was later consummated on the IRC's initiative—though with limitations which substantially reduced the scope of the original proposals. In addition, some of the very large mergers promoted by the IRC clearly created major monopoly situations: it seems unlikely, for example, that if the GEC/AEI/EE series of mergers had ever been referred to the Monopolies Commission that they would have been allowed to proceed.

Extended use of the Monopolies Commission inevitably gave greater discretionary powers to the Board of Trade, since it was left to the Board to decide what matters to refer to the Commission and then to decide what action, if any, it would take upon the Commission's recommendations. In the event, the Board has shown considerable willingness to persuade or force companies to follow the recommendations of the Commission. One interesting example was the action which followed the Commission's report on household detergents. The main recommendations were that the manufacturers of these detergents should cut their advertising expenditures by forty per cent and lower their prices.* Eight months after the appearance of the report, and following a massive series of consultations with the industry, the President of the Board of Trade announced that the manufacturers had rejected the proposed cut in advertising spending, but they were to freeze their prices for two years and would introduce a new range of products at prices twenty per cent below those of their existing range. These lower priced 'State soaps', as they have been derisively called, have been a market failure. Despite their lower prices housewives have largely refused to buy them—an interesting sidelight on how theoretical logic can go astray in the market economy.

Just as expansion of Monopolies Commission activity has given increased discretionary powers to the Board of Trade, so has the Prices and Incomes policy given various Ministries greatly enhanced opportunities for selective intervention. The Policy has always operated on the basis of Departments using their discretion on the matters which they choose to refer to the National Board for Prices and Incomes, and then using it again in determining what action they will take following the Board's reports.

* HC Paper, Session 1966–1967, No. 105.

Just as nobody would suggest deliberate abuse of the Board of Trade's powers under the Monopolies legislation, so nobody would expect to see abuse of the discretionary powers given to ministers under the Prices and Incomes Policy. The fact is, however, that both these sets of operations have enormously enhanced the discretionary powers of ministers. They have vastly extended the area in which intervention takes place, not in direct and automatic operation of the law, but on what may seem to be an arbitrary whim of the minister. This massive expansion of discretionary powers has both psychological and practical consequences. Psychologically, ministerial powers to pick and choose between apparently similar cases could inevitably cause feelings of resentment and unfair treatment among those affected. In practical terms, doubts about whether or not some minister or other may decide to intervene adds one more substantial element of uncertainty to the environment in which industry has to operate. The existence of agencies like the IRC, with virtually unfettered powers of intervention, adds yet another element of uncertainty. As we shall see in later chapters, accumulated resentments and mounting uncertainty simply do not create the climate in which desirable activities like expansion, modernisation, and innovation burgeon.

CHAPTER SEVEN

Legislation for intervention

Despite the brave efforts of Mr Hugh Gaitskill to woo the Labour Party away from Clause 4 of its constitution, nationalisation remains an article of faith for Party zealots. Renationalisation of steel had long been one of the proclaimed aims of the party, and this duly appeared in the 1964 Manifesto, though—possibly because opinion polls had shown 'nationalisation' to be unpopular—it was presented under the euphemism of replacing 'private monopoly' in the steel industry by 'public ownership and control'.* 'Public ownership' of the water supply industry was also promised, and in 1968 details were announced of long-mooted proposals to nationalise most of Britain's docks. Steel and water supply have been duly nationalised. If the docks follow, the Labour Government will, since 1964, have added £1,000 million of assets to those already held by the public sector.

These measures are sometimes dismissed by sophisticated Labour spokesmen as the party's last fling in 'old-style' nationalisation. This may be true, but it is little consolation to those who believe in the market economy, or to those who believe in a mixed economy in which manufacture, as distinct from the provision of monopoly services, is a free enterprise activity. The addition of steel, water supply, and the docks to the public sector puts yet another large slice of the economy under direct Government control.

This, however, has only been a starting point in the Labour Government's moves to put ever widening segments of the economy into the hands of State Corporations. The period 1964–68 has been notable for a variety of measures to promote the interests of the State Corporations at the expense of private enterprise interests, and to extend the role of the Public Corporations by the process familiarly known as 'creeping nationalisation'.

NATIONALISED STEEL

The weighting of the scales against private enterprise can be clearly seen in some of the actions of the Government and the British Steel Corporation since nationalisation. In November 1968 the British

* Labour Party Election Manifesto, 1964 and 1966.

Steel Corporation proposed a new price structure which would provide for price increases totalling £56·5 million in a full year. The proposed price increases would constitute a heavy burden on a number of British industries, notably shipbuilding. The Corporation's application was referred to the National Board for Prices and Incomes, whose report is awaited at the time of writing.

A most evident effect of the new price structure would be to cause great hardship to the remaining privately owned sector of the British iron and steel industry, since above average price increases were sought for semi-finished steels which the private sector buys in substantial quantity for re-rolling and finishing. *The Times* has reported that private steel makers have asked that a new Government body should be appointed to oversee steel prices, and have requested that the Prices and Incomes Board should support the proposal.*

Another form of discrimination against the private steel makers has been the Government's action with regard to import duties on crude and semi-finished steels. From 1 January 1969, the British Steel Corporation was granted a temporary exemption from such duty on crude and semi-finished steel imports. No such exemption was granted to the private sector, subjecting it to a nine per cent penalty relative to the British Steel Corporation.

THE TRANSPORT ACT

The more controversial provisions of the Transport Act 1968, have yet to be implemented, but they provide for substantial discrimination against private enterprise industry. The most obvious interventionist provisions arise from changes in the licensing of commercial road vehicles. The present system of A and B licences for public carriers and C licences for operators of their own vehicles to carry their own goods, are to be scrapped. Licences will be granted for vehicles up to sixteen tons gross weight subject to certain standards of maintenance, operation, and management being met. Operators of goods vehicles over sixteen tons gross weight will have to apply to the Licensing Authority for the right to provide a service, and the new National Freight Corporation will have the right to object on the grounds that the service or part of it could be provided wholly or partly by rail. Although there are some clauses providing that speed, reliability and cost, the nature of the goods and the needs of the person for whom the goods are to be carried, are to be taken into account by the Licensing Authority, the clear intention of the Act is to force traffic away from road haulage to the nationalised railway system.

This is self-evidently the blatant intervention of State control into industry, carrying the threat that vital commercial considerations

* *The Times*, 8 April 1969.

will be overridden to give a boost to the fortunes of British Rail. Transport costs, and speed and reliability in the transport of goods are crucial to industrial efficiency. With road transport costs already inflated by almost continuous increases in taxation, the road haulage sector already suffers from a high degree of State discrimination. The new licensing provisions, when they are brought into effect, will add a big twist to the Government's attempts to force industry into the use of transport services which it would not voluntarily choose on the grounds of real cost or convenience.

Another effect of the Transport Act has been the writing-off of the huge capital debts of the nationalised railways and waterways. The disappearance of some £1,200 million of accumulated debt is primarily a political manoeuvre. On the one hand it removes the constant reminder to the public of the losses run up by these organisations since nationalisation. At the same time it gives the railways and the waterways a new chance to break-even financially, and thus shed the stigma of continuous loss-making which could hardly have been beneficial to the image of nationalisation. It does not, of course, relieve the tax-payer of any of the burdens of interest he has had to carry as a result of the accumulating losses to the railways. The interest still has to be met.

The same principle of writing-off accumulated debt has been applied to the National Coal Board. Another variant, the institution of 'State Equity Capital', has been tried with the British Overseas Airways Corporation, and the British Steel Corporation is reputed to be anxious to dispose of much of its fixed interest capital burden, resulting from nationalisation and subsequent losses, by resorting to the same type of 'Equity'. The essence of the 'State Equity' idea is that the nationalised Corporations favoured by this type of financing will pay dividends to the Treasury when they can afford them, but be exempt from interest payments on the finances concerned in years in which they make losses or inadequate profits.

CREEPING NATIONALISATION

Among developments in the nationalised sector which private industry views with the gravest disquiet are provisions successively made by the Government to enable State Corporations to encroach on increasing sectors of industrial activity. This was promised in Labour's 1964–66 election manifestoes, on the grounds that the restrictions of the nationalised industries to the purposes for which they were originally created was 'illogical'. Subsequent legislation has given virtually limitless powers to the State Corporations to move into new sectors of industry, and, of course, to compete with private companies already operating in such sectors.

The Coal Industry Act 1965, empowered the National Coal Board to borrow from the Ministers of Power for *acquiring an undertaking or part of an undertaking* and *subscribing for or acquiring shares, stock debentures, debenture stock, or other securities of a like nature, of a body corporate, otherwise by way of investment*. The Transport Act 1968, gave the Railways Board, the Waterways Board, and the various other authorities being established wide powers to manufacture and trade. The Waterways Board, for example, is allowed to sell *goods of any description to outside persons, whether or not persons using their waterways, at any place where persons using those waterways may require facilities for the purchase of those goods*. Slightly less comprehensive facilities were granted to the other State Boards and Corporations set up in the Transport Act in so far as some of them were limited to using materials or facilities or skills already existing in common with some existing activity.

In addition to these special powers granted to the outstanding loss-making sectors of the nationalised industries, other nationalised corporations, such as the airlines, have been encouraged to use powers to develop new enterprises, sometimes in partnership with private enterprise companies, and sometimes involving the taking over of existing private enterprises.

The reasoning behind the massive scope for new encroachments into private industry given to the State Corporations is both economic and political. On the economic side, the Government has argued that the public sector should not be confined to declining activities which are likely to incur overall loss on trading operations, but should be free to exploit new opportunities where the skills and expertise to be found within the public sector can be put to profitable advantage. On the political side expansion of the nationalised sector of industry has for long been Labour Party dogma, while securing some new profitable activities to offset losses on traditional activities has obvious attractions in improving the image of the coal and railway industries.

It is not surprising that the vast scope provided for extension of the activities of the public sector has caused considerable resentment and alarm in private industry. Companies clearly face the threat of subsidised competition. As experience of the nationalised industries has for long shown, their losses are automatically met by the tax-payer. Under the measures which Labour has introduced there seems little check on the State Corporations borrowing money at favourable terms from the Government, moving into competition with private companies, and then having their losses guaranteed if they prove unsuccessful. Such a course of events would obviously be harmful to the economy, and in the process efficient private companies could suffer substantial loss through having to meet this artificially financed competition.

The sweeping new powers granted to the nationalised industries have not so far been put to very extensive use, nor have any cases of abuse yet come to light. Inevitably, however, the existence of these powers adds to the uncertainty under which the private sector of industry has had to labour throughout the Government's term of office. It is unreasonable to expect private companies to invest funds in expansion if they have to be continually looking over their shoulders expecting some State-subsidised competitor to enter their spheres of activity. In psychological terms, they are also not likely to be stimulated by the thought that the taxes they pay are going to help the new competitor to compete with them.

THE INDUSTRIAL EXPANSION ACT

Apart from these measures of overt nationalisation and the powers given to the existing public sector to extend its activities at will, the Government has also taken powers which effectively allow it to acquire private enterprise companies without even the formality of full Parliamentary debate. As we have seen, such powers were indirectly acquired when the Industrial Reorganisation Corporation was set up. The idea of the Corporation was attacked by critics at the time as a means of 'backdoor nationalisation'. Such criticisms were dismissed by Government spokesmen although the proposed legislation quite clearly gave the Corporation powers to purchase majority or total stakes in companies. The critics have duly been proved right, in the sense that the company Brown Bayley was purchased by the Industrial Reorganisation Corporation early in 1969. It is likely that the company will be split into constituent parts and the steel-making interests sold off to the British Steel Corporation, and other interests offered to private enterprise companies in merger deals. In principle, however, there would be nothing to stop the Industrial Reorganisation Corporation from taking over a company at will and subjecting it indefinitely to whatever wishes any Government Department might express towards it.

All the suspicions voiced about the Industrial Reorganisation Corporation were redoubled when the Government introduced the Industrial Expansion Bill and White Paper in January 1968.* The essence of the Bill was that it gave powers to Government Departments, notably the Ministry of Technology and the Department of Economic Affairs, to use massive Government finance—up to £150 million in the first instance, for virtually any industrial purpose they deemed desirable. The purposes could include the purchase of

* HC Bills, 1967–68, No. 65; Cmnd 3509.

companies, or the setting up of new State industrial ventures. The Bill was simply enabling legislation, permitting the Government a free hand in industry with no more formality than the lodging of statutory instruments before Parliament—in effect Ministers could go on the take-over trail, or could set up new industrial enterprises, without even the need for full debate in Parliament. The alleged justification for these sweeping powers was the supposed existence of industrial projects which would be beneficial to the nation but would not be pursued by commercial interests because they would not be sufficiently profitable.

The sweeping powers taken in the Industrial Expansion Act have so far been put to very limited use. It is indeed a jibe of the Government's political opponents that the merger of International Computers and Tabulators and the data processing interests of English Electric was held back by the Government so that financial help could be given under the Act and thus substantiate the claim that the legislation had been necessary! The existence of these powers, however, clearly occasions disquiet and uncertainty to private enterprise companies.

The period under review, then, has seen a major increase in the nationalised sector, the removal of many existing restrictions on its growth, and the introduction of legislation which could effectively enable the Government to nationalise substantial undertakings at will. Whatever else these dogmatically socialist measures have done, they have hardly increased the confidence of free enterprise industry, nor have they helped to promote the 'partnership' between industry and Government for which Labour politicians in their more conciliatory moments call.

CHAPTER EIGHT

What went wrong?

It is a matter of factual history that in economic terms the period from Labour's election victory on 15 October 1964 to the end of 1968 was one of the most disastrous in post-1945 experience.

Instead of the promised acceleration in economic growth, the rate of increase in Gross Domestic Product fell by nearly a quarter. Over the four years 1960–64 the rate of annual increase was three and a quarter per cent; between 1964 and 1968 it was around two and a half per cent, calculated in each case from output.

In terms of individual prosperity, the record is even more dismal. The all-items index of retail prices rose nineteen per cent between 1964 and 1968. Personal disposable income, at constant prices, grew by 2·7 per cent a year between 1960 and 1964, while it had grown by three per cent annually in the thirteen years 1951–64. Between 1964 and 1968 it grew at only one and a half per cent annually.* This fall in the rate of growth of personal prosperity was matched by an even sharper fall in the rate of growth of personal saving, from five per cent a year between 1960–64 to 1·9 per cent between 1964–68,* leading to talk of a flight from cash into goods. Taxation was increased by £2,625 million over the period.

In industrial terms, the record was equally disastrous. Industrial output grew at only 2·15 per cent a year between 1964 and 1968, compared with 3·3 per cent average annual growth during the previous four years. Fixed investment in manufacturing industry, which Labour had hoped to stimulate, barely exceeded, at constant prices, the levels achieved as far back as 1961.

Overshadowing everything else in the Government's economic priorities was the achievement of external balance. In fact, only in two uncharacteristic quarters between 1964 and the end of 1968 was a balance of payments surplus achieved. The pound was devalued in November 1967. The 1968 deficit, despite the advantages of devaluation and a quite exceptional boom in world trade, was £458 million. Britain's overseas debts rose by over £2,000 million during the period, mostly due for repayment by the early 'seventies.

* Parliamentary Answer, *Hansard*, 4 March 1969.

WHAT WENT WRONG? 75

Such a record is a grotesque caricature of the hopes Labour pinned on economic planning and industrial intervention in 1964, and certainly of the expectations it then aroused among electors.

WHAT CAUSED THIS DEBACLE?

A number of explanations has been put forward, varying, as might be expected, with the political allegiances of those concerned. Labour leaders for some years vociferously blamed their 'inheritance', implying that only the balance of payments deficit left by the outgoing Conservative administration had frustrated their plans. Opponents of the regime have consistently made accusations of general economic mismanagement, leading to accelerating loss of confidence both at home and overseas. Soaring levels of public expenditure and failure to check rising personal consumption effectively have also been incriminated, while more sophisticated explanations suggest that failure to control the money supply or to devalue the pound before November 1967 were primarily to blame for collapse of the growth expectations which Labour had fostered.

It would be beyond the scope of this book to attempt a general appraisal of the Labour Government's economic policies during the period under study. One explanation for the almost unrelieved succession of failures is now being put forward, however, which is absolutely germane to our theme. It was phrased as follows in the Labour Party's 'mid-term manifesto' prepared for the 1968 Conference: *In fact what we are seeing now in 1968 is the revival of the British economy which we had hoped to achieve by 1966. Production is now going up, the nation's regional balance is being improved, productivity is reaching new levels and the prospects for Britain's trade are better than at any point in a decade. All of this is the result of firm action taken earlier to achieve industrial modernisation and reconstruction—to bring about a transformation of the debilitated economic structure we inherited into one capable of responding to, and taking advantage of the technological revolution through which the world is living.**

Put another way (and in the terms in which it will doubtless be phrased as the next General Election approaches) the claim is that the spate of intervention in the economy and in industry between 1964 and 1968 has laid the foundations for an economic miracle which will appear at some unspecified time in the future.

This is manifestly an absolutely crucial contention. If it is correct all the nation has to do is to co-operate with due zeal in pursuit of the policies which the Government has laid down, and to await the promised, if long-delayed, upsurge in prosperity. If the contention is

* *Britain: Progress and Change*, Labour Party, September 1968.

fundamentally false, however, and if, as many critics insist, much of the Government's effort during the last four years has been either an irrelevance or a handicap to industry, then we must expect continuance or possibly worsening of our present troubles.

In the ensuing chapters, which constitute the second part of this book, we attempt to evaluate as objectively as possible the effects which the measures outlined in the previous chapters have so far brought. From this base it is possible to predict what future results a continuance of the various measures and policies will achieve, making due allowance for the fact that the payoff of political and economic measures is often long delayed.

Before we move on to this detailed enquiry there are a number of general points which should be made. One of the difficulties in any economic assessment is to deduce a real relationship between cause and effect. This is a difficulty which will obtrude frequently in our enquiry, since it is obviously the case that a great deal of progress takes place in industry because of the working of normal economic forces with Government actions playing a negligible part as causal factors. Sometimes, indeed, industry progresses in spite of rather than because of Government policies. It has long been the custom for Governments of all political complexions to claim the credit for any beneficial changes which occurred during their periods of office, while denying as far as possible responsibility for any adverse happenings. In the following chapters the benefit of the doubt is given to Government measures where it seems reasonable to do so, but it is important to bear in mind that a very large proportion of the industrial restructuring, technological advance, capital investment, productivity bargaining, etc., which has taken place over the period would have occurred almost irrespective of what policies the Government was pursuing. Failure to bear in mind industry's own capacity to achieve beneficial progress can only result in unwisely overestimating the capacity of politicians and civil servants to alter the course of economic events.

Another difficulty which obtrudes is that of semantics. There is scope for a good deal of argument over what constitutes success or failure for economic policies. After Britain's traumatic experiences since 1964 it seems likely that any movement into balance of payments stability, however small, will be hailed by many observers (and particularly by Labour politicians) as a major economic success, if not as an economic miracle. While this is understandable in political terms, it would be no service to any public discussion of Britain's future to accept such minimal standards. It has always been obvious that Britain could achieve a surplus if the people's living standards were depressed sufficiently. To be meaningful to the community as a whole, economic success would imply not only balance of payments stability, taking one year with another, but genuine economic growth, including growth in disposable incomes, of at least the order implied in Mr George Brown's abortive National Plan.

Are we, in fact to use the Labour Party's own words, seeing a *revival of the British economy*? 1968 was undoubtedly an improvement after the virtual stagnation of 1966 and 1967, but at mid-March 1969, few commentators were prepared to suggest that the year's balance of payments targets would be met, let alone that substantial economic growth would be achieved.

The *Sunday Times* was summing up the situation in the following terms: *After sixteen months of a* $2.40 *parity, the £ is once more hovering round its low point and the subject of substantial Bank of England support. Bank Rate is back to its crisis level of eight per cent, and could easily go higher. Building society mortgage rates have moved to their highest peak in history. The chances of our making any substantial dent in the £500 million international debt bill which falls due in the course of 1969 are rapidly diminishing and the odds on a first-class monetary crisis this year, with inevitably unpleasant consequences for sterling, look as firm, or firmer than ever.**

Even the much-respected National Institute of Economic and Social Research commented: *The year following devaluation has clearly been disappointing. The improvement in the balance of payments was slow and hesitant, and at the end of the year the outlook for the further future still seemed far from reassuring.*† It warned sombrely: *For the medium term, it is realistic to think of most of the major devaluation effects having worked themselves out by the end of this year. The chances of any marked further improvement in the balance of payments after this year therefore seem correspondingly small.*

Such commentators may be proved wrong, of course, as economic forecasters (including Government forecasters) have been proved wrong before. For what such views are worth, however, they do little to suggest authoritative support for the contention that an economic 'miracle' is on the way for Britain—sometime—as a result of Labour's action between 1964 and 1968.

The same conclusion, indeed, tends to emerge if the *firm action taken earlier to achieve industrial modernisation and reconstruction* is considered. In the ensuing chapters we describe in detail the fruits of Labour's interventions in various industrial matters which it claimed to be crucial. What we shall find is that in spite of almost innumerable Government sorties into the industrial and economic arena, the sum total of results falls far short of anything which could truthfully

---

* *Sunday Times*, 16 March 1969.
† *National Institute Economic Review*, No. 47, February 1969.

be described as a significant 'reconstruction'. The situation is rather like that of the over-enthusiastic car owner who has tinkered with everything in sight, without ever accomplishing a major overhaul of his vehicle.

To take some specific sectors which Labour rightly regarded as of supreme importance, the promised 'technical revolution' was nowhere in sight in mid-1968, according to the authoritative Brookings Institution,* nor could it be expected because there had been no shift of resources sufficient to cause anything 'revolutionary' to occur. Of course, there had been occasional technological triumphs, such as the American orders for the Rolls-Royce RB211 engine, but it would be difficult to claim that they were occurring on a greater scale than in non-interventionist days. There may equally have been some acceleration in British industry's adoption of advanced techniques, but it was much too modest to alter the international competitive balance.

The same picture of minimal results from a mass of interventionist effort emerges in other sectors. Regional policies may have made a miniscule contribution to spreading employment into Britain's less-prosperous regions, while some new investment has undoubtedly been attracted or forced into locations which would not otherwise have been adopted: the price, however, has been considerable economic distortion, and the abandonment or deferral of expansion which would otherwise have taken place. There is no evidence at all that 'under-used resources' have been brought into employment to provide economic growth which would otherwise not have occurred.

It is unquestionably the case that a great many mergers have taken place in British industry during Labour's term of office, particularly during 1967 and 1968. Most of this movement has been industry's response to economic forces, and it is probably true to suggest that many of the mergers which did occur with Government help would have taken place if it had not in fact been available. This merger movement can reasonably be regarded as a substantial restructuring of industry and some of it, though by no means all, should produce useful results in terms of rationalisation and scale economies in due course, but it would be a misuse of words to suggest that this will represent a revolutionary advance on the progress which has been made in these fields in British industry over the last decade. Benefits from the merger movement are likely to be considerably offset by the fact that in most cases mergers have been undertaken as an alternative to new capital investment, as Chapter 12 shows.

The crucial failure in Labour's plans lies in this field of capital

* *Britain's Economic Prospects*, Brookings Institution, 1968, p. 448.

investment. Where the country needed at least a rise in manufacturing investment levels to those of its international competitors, what has occurred has been a decline to below the standard achieved in 1961. At the end of 1968 many companies were reporting capacity shortages, and it seemed certain that if the promised 'economic revival' were in fact to occur, it would soon be cut short through lack of resources to produce the required goods. At the same time, hundreds of millions of pounds of resources, which should have gone into productive capacity, modernisation, and innovation, have gone elsewhere—into high taxation and high interest charges, into inflationary cost rises, and soaring public expenditure.

In face of this situation it seems, to put it mildly, extravagant to claim that the foundations have been laid for an economic revival in any meaningful sense of the term. It would be equally extravagant to suggest that the psychological basis for vigorous economic growth has been achieved. Chapter 13 suggests that the years 1964–68 have produced mounting disillusionment and growing frustration at increasing intervention and bureaucracy.

THE CREDIBILITY OF INTERVENTION

If this is a fair assessment of the overall results of four years of determined and growing intervention, it is pertinent to ask why the hopes of the Labour Party and its supporters have been so sadly belied. One explanation, of course, lies in the difficulties of achieving external balance which have best beset the Government throughout its period of office. It can reasonably be argued that if Labour had inherited at least a neutral balance of payment situation and had consequently not been forced to pursue policies of mounting 'austerity', it would have been correspondingly easier to achieve an appropriate diversion of resources to such things as technology and manufacturing investment. There is, however, a good deal that is circular in such an argument, for it must be the case that if the Government had been able to achieve its proclaimed ambitions in industry and technology, then the balance of payments difficulties should have speedily melted away.

What seems to have been at least a contributory cause of all the disappointments suffered since 1964 is that Labour politicians, and particularly the economic theorists from whom they draw their inspiration, vastly over-rated the results which political intervention in industry could achieve. In the euphoria of 1964 and 1965 it was too readily assumed that a few hundred intelligent chaps in Whitehall, backed by a few hundred million pounds of Government money and a Parliamentary majority passing the right legislation could somehow achieve the transformation of British industry which had eluded the previous generation of industrialists and politicians. The main lesson, from all that has subsequently transpired, is perhaps that the industry of an advanced nation is much too complex to permit of such simplistic solutions.

There have been some modest straws in the wind to suggest that Labour is beginning to learn this lesson. They include Mr Callaghan's plea that the compulsory elements in Incomes Policy should not be continued beyond 1969, but the main evidence that Labour has been chastened by its experience of intervention comes from its 1968-69 approach to national economic planning. Contrast the diffidence with which the 1969 'planning document'* was presented with the ballyhoo which surrounded the 1965 National Plan, and there is fairly conclusive proof of loss of faith in the proposition that a few masterminds given adequate powers in Whitehall could fairly easily solve all our difficulties.

Another reaction to the apparent overall failure of intervention is to claim that there has not been enough of it, or that it has been too widely spread over too many objectives. This is broadly the claim of Labour's extreme Left, which argues for more nationalisation and more controls. On a highly selective basis the view has some support from more moderate sources: the Brookings Institution has, for example, argued that if a technical revolution was really to be brought about it would require a much more deliberate and substantial concentration of resources than has so far been attempted.† It can be similarly argued that if the aim is to increase capital investment then bigger and more effective incentives are required from public funds.

The credibility of some of these propositions is examined in the following chapters, which attempt to assess in detail the effects of the major measures of intervention adopted by the Labour Government. While this investigation reveals some modest successes—and it would be surprising if such a huge interventionist effort had no success at all to record—what tends to emerge with great frequency is the extent to which unwanted and often unexpected side effects tend to outweigh whatever benefits intervention has brought. Any reasonable understanding of the complex inter-relationships which make up a modern industrial society would lead one to expect that intervention at any one point in the economy would produce reactions, some of them highly undesirable, at innumerable other points. The more powerful and concentrated the intervention, the greater the 'economic distortions'. It is perhaps this factor, more than any other, which has tended to frustrate the high hopes of interventionists

* *The Task Ahead*, DEA, 1969, HMSO.
† Op. cit., Chapter 8.

over the last few years and which has eroded the faith in what a well-intentioned Whitehall could achieve in industry which was such a feature of the British political scene before these assumed powers were actually put to the test.

CHAPTER NINE

The effects of tax changes

We examined in Chapter 3 the various measures which followed Labour's 1946 promise to use tax policies *to encourage the right type of modern industry*.* These included the precipitate and ill-considered introduction of a Corporation Tax which penalised distribution of profits; a long-term Capital Gains Tax; increasing tax discrimination against overseas investment by British companies and British citizens: disallowance of all business entertainment (except the entertainment of overseas buyers) as an expense allowable against taxation, and numerous other measures intended to eliminate or minimise tax avoidance; increasing tax discrimination against service industries and service functions in manufacturing industry, including the controversial Selective Employment Tax, and discriminatory elements in investment grants; and an attempt to discourage imports by the Imports Deposits Scheme. The last two of these measures exact forced loans from industry and business together approaching nearly £1,000 million.

We also saw in Chapter 3 that since Labour came to office in October 1964, it had increased the taxation imposed on the community by £2,625 million a year—a rate of tax increase entirely unprecedented in British peace-time history. In addition, for most of the period 1965–68 an intensifying credit squeeze was under way and increasingly stringent hire-purchase restrictions were enforced.

Both the soaring tax burden and the restrictions on credit were imposed in the name of 'management of the economy'. As we saw in Chapter 8, none of the significant statistics for the period suggests that such 'management' was beneficial.

Our purpose in this chapter is to endeavour to elucidate the effects on British industry of the tax 'reforms' and of the escalating taxation burden on companies and individual citizens.

LABOUR'S THEORIES

When the Government took office in October 1964 it had a number of perfectly praiseworthy industrial objectives. It sought faster economic

* Labour Party Manifesto, 1964.

growth, the modernisation of British industry's capital stock, more rapid technological innovation, and improvement of the trade balance through greater export competitiveness and import substitution.

It had proclaimed, and no doubt genuinely believed, that changes in the tax system could help to achieve all these aims. The crucial factor was seen to be capital investment, which throughout the post-1945 period had in Britain lagged behind our major international trade competitors.

When it came to the point of translating its aims into tax practice, the Labour Government—or, to be more accurate, the then Chancellor of the Exchequer, Mr James Callaghan—decided to adopt virtually lock, stock, and barrel, the theories held by Professor Nicholas Kaldor and put forward by him in a note of dissent to the 1954 Report of the Royal Commission on Taxation. This was a remarkable intrusion of a single individual into Britain's whole system of company taxation, which has been the subject of an enormous amount of critical comment.* The essence of Professor Kaldor's theories can be roughly summarised as follows. The determining factor in investment decisions is the availability of liquid resources. The tax system should therefore be used to encourage retention of profits and thus to discourage dividend distributions. The way to achieve this aim was sharply differentiated taxation on distributed and non-distributed profits. The actual mechanism was to be a corporation tax which would be paid on the whole profits of the company and which should be set at a substantially lower level than the combined income tax and profits tax level to which companies were subject in 1964. Dividend payments, on the other hand, should be treated as new income and bear full income tax and surtax on their way to the recipient. It was seen that increasing retentions would lead to a steady rise in the capital value of companies and this constituted a supporting justification for the introduction of a long term Capital Gains Tax. In fact, there can be little doubt that Labour would in any case have introduced such a tax as a matter of equity, especially as the Conservatives had already conceded the case for taxing capital gains.

There were a number of additions to this basic theory which enshrined some traditional Labour prejudices. It was traditional in the Party, for example, to regard investment by British companies overseas as less desirable than domestic investment. Overseas investment was regarded as adding only remitted profits to the Gross National Product, whereas with domestic investment the whole

* See, for example, *British Industry Week*, 7 March 1969, 'The Scandal of Tax Dictatorship'.

output was an accretion to national wealth which could either be exported or would save imports. In addition domestic investment provided jobs for British working men while overseas investment only created jobs for foreigners. This traditional bias against overseas investment was naturally enough enhanced by the balance of payments situation which Labour inherited: reducing the outflow of British capital would contribute to reduction of the overseas deficit.

Another prejudice long characteristic of the Labour Party which was enshrined in the tax system during 1966 was the belief that service industries are of less value to the nation than manufacturing. The usual supporting argument for such a view is that manufactures provide export earnings while services do not—though such an assertion has to ignore or treat as an exception, Britain's big overseas earnings in invisibles. A more esoteric justification for discrimination against service industries was put forward by Professor Kaldor in his inaugural lecture at Cambridge University in 1967.* His thesis was that growth of manufacturing industry was held back by labour shortages which resulted from the absorption of potential employees into service industries; holding back the growth of service industries, or at least deterring the trend towards increasing employment within them, would release manpower for growth of manufacturing industry.

In addition to incorporating these various theoretical elements, Labour's tax policies in the 1965–66 'reforms' also constituted an attack on one other villain in traditional party mythology: whatever else might happen as a result, the investor (usually referred to as a 'speculator' in party propaganda) could be expected to be worse off. If companies toed the expected line and retained more of their profits, investors' dividend income would suffer, while any resulting capital gains would be taxed; if companies proved recalcitrant and increased their dividends, then investment income would be caught in a form of double taxation which would substantially reduce its after-tax value.

All the theories which Mr Callaghan so uncritically embraced are open [to considerable dispute. While company investment policies are, of course, dependent upon access to liquid resources, there is no reliable correlation between company retentions and economically desirable capital investment. Companies with conservative dividend policies may either rush off into unrewarding diversification activities or simply sit on increasing cash reserves. Money available for investment is at least as likely to be put to maximum economic use by its

* Kaldor, N., *Causes of the Slow Rate of Economic Growth of the United Kingdom: An Inaugural Lecture* (Cambridge University Press, 1967).

distribution to investors and recirculation through the capital markets as it is through retention in company coffers.

Arguments over the value to the nation of company investment overseas have raged for many years. They have not been greatly clarified by the two Reddaway Reports commissioned by the Confederation of British Industry, which, despite the enormous academic effort involved, seem to have adopted too narrow a base and to ignore one of the most important elements in the operations of international oil industry. One important point, however, emerges from a major recent study of Britain's Balance of Payments. The National Recovery Programme Research Paper No. 3* showed that achievement of a perennial surplus on Britain's balance of external trade was extremely unlikely: steadily growing returns from overseas investment were essential to achieve overall external balance in view of our historic propensity to run a continuing deficit on visible trading account.

The arguments deployed to justify discrimination in service industries are equally open to scepticism. In particular, the suggestion that British manufacturing industry suffers from a basic shortage of labour is laughed at by management consultants, who instead suggest that the besetting sin of British companies is 'concealed unemployment' resulting from the employment of unnecessarily large numbers by comparison with those of our international competitors. Estimates for overmanning vary from twenty per cent to thirty per cent of the number employed in British industry; such figures are only well-informed guesses, but they suggest that at least 5,000,000 people could be released for productive work if concealed unemployment were effectively tackled!

There is, in fact, plenty of scope for arguing that the theories which Labour so precipitately enshrined in tax practice in 1965–66 are all at least in the non-proven category. No attempt was made before the tax 'reforms' were introduced to conduct any kind of empirical investigation of the underlying theories, nor were adequate consultations held on the principles of the proposed reforms with bodies who might be expected to have informed views on their value. In the space of two years Britain was thus saddled with a new system of corporate taxation whose sole justification was the view of one academic economist and those of a handful of party zealots.

TAX THEORIES IN ACTION

The period since Mr Callaghan's taxation 'reforms' in 1965–66 has been so studded with deflationary budgetary measures, soaring general levels of taxation, credit squeezes and statutory limitations

* A Programme for National Recovery, Research Paper No. 3. *The Balance of Payments and Invisible Earnings*, London, January 1969.

COMPAN

	1957	1958	19
Income			
Income earned in the United Kingdom:			
Gross trading profits of companies*†	3,075	2,983	3,3
Rent and non-trading income..	712	745	7
Total	3,787	3,728	4,0
Income earned abroad§	870	960	9
Total	4,657	4,688	5,0
Allocation of income			
Dividends and interest:			
Payments:			
Debenture and loan interest	75	85	
Dividends on preference shares	109	108	1
Dividends on ordinary shares	645	690	8
Co-operative society dividends and interest ..	60	59	
Interest on building society shares and deposits ..	101	108	1
Other interest paid by banks, etc...	95	104	
Total payments of dividends and interest ..	1,085	1,154	1,2
Additions to dividend reserves	27	72	1
Current transfers to charities	12	13	
Profits due abroad net of United Kingdom tax§ ..	142	158	1
United Kingdom taxes on income:			
Payments on profits due abroad	62	67	
Payments on other profits	888	922	8
Additions to reserves on profits due abroad ..	−6	17	
Additions to reserves on other profits	56	−136	−2
Taxes paid abroad	348	353	4
Balance: undistributed income after taxation but before providing for depreciation and stock appreciation..	2,043	2,068	2,2
Total	4,657	4,688	5,0

* Before providing for depreciation and stock appreciation.
† Including United Kingdom branches and subsidiaries of non-resident parent comp;
‡ After deducting payments of selective employment tax and before allowing for refur
premiums due but not yet received.
§ After deducting depreciation allowances but before providing for stock appreciati

PROPRIATION ACCOUNT

£ million

60	1961	1962	1963	1964	1965	1966	1967
39	3,646	3,599	4,113	4,616	4,820	3,513‡	4,694‡
50	917	913	929	1,065	1,236	1,359	1,476
89	4,563	4,512	5,042	5,681	6,056	5,872	6,170
49	975	1,073	1,151	1,300	1,453	1,401	1,433
38	5,538	5,585	6,193	6,981	7,509	7,273	7,603
07	120	157	172	185	212	300	369
12	117	119	119	124	121	117	112
40	1,185	1,180	1,320	1,520	1,735	1,715	1,630
58	57	54	52	50	50	47	47
27	149	172	184	211	265	311	370
34	159	137	128	186	260	311	321
78	1,787	1,819	1,975	2,276	2,643	2,801	2,849
63	55	75	161	45	10	−71	80
17	19	21	24	26	28	30	32
79	143	159	190	227	247	210	230
91	119	131	118	135	163	198	159
12	682	842	733	569	492	501	863
40	−4	2	39	73	−2	−69	−13
77	108	−152	−60	233	25	458	272
59	394	422	420	512	552	543	551
12	2,235	2,266	2,593	2,885	3,351	2,672	2,580
38	5,538	5,585	6,193	6,981	7,509	7,273	7,603

Source: Central Statistical Office

on price and dividend increases that it is impossible to trace a precise connection between the 'reforms' and the subsequent course of events.

In crude terms, however, the available evidence suggests that the basic theories underlying the tax changes were shown to be unfounded once they were put into action. One of the crucial assumptions was that a harsh differential tax rate on distributed profits would encourage retentions. The table on pp. 86 and 87 shows that in 1967, after the 'reforms' had been instituted, undistributed profits of British companies fell to their lowest level since 1962; the proportion of gross income retained fell to the historically low level of 34·2 per cent from levels of 41·4 per cent in 1964 and 44·7 per cent in 1965 under the old company tax system. The table strongly suggests that the reasons for the sharp drop in retentions were escalating taxation and higher debenture and loan interest—both, of course, the fruit of Government policies. Dividend distributions remained virtually stable, at around 21 per cent of gross company income, from 1964 to 1967.

Manufacturing investment failed to achieve the hoped for growth. At constant (1958) prices it was £1,195 million in 1961, £1,203 million in 1965, £1,233 million in 1966, and back to £1,176 million in 1967. There are a number of explanations for this disappointing performance (see Chapter 12), but one is of interest here because it seems to have been an unconvenanted consequence of the 'reforms' of 1965–66. While industrial capital investment was continuing at a depressingly low level in 1967 and 1968, there was an unprecedented boom in mergers and takeovers in British industry. One reason for this was that industrialists had come to the conclusion that this type of activity was likely to prove a safer and more profitable outlet for investment funds, in the depressing economic climate of the times, than physical expansion. In addition, Mr Callaghan's 'reforms' had made mergers and takeovers an increasingly attractive proposition for both the bid-for and the bidder. Capital gains tax meant that shareholders were reluctant to take cash and realise a gain, and were consequently happy to have their shares taken over for another company's 'paper'. Thus bidders could make takeover proposals without the inconvenience of having to raise cash, and the attractions were increased by the fact that share values moved sharply upwards after the introduction of Corporation Tax.

This was another uncovenanted effect of Mr Callaghan's 'reforms'. The tax bias against dividends made companies reluctant to raise finance by equity issues; as they turned to debentures and loan stocks, an increasing shortage of ordinary shares, relative to demand, inevitably helped to push up Stock Exchange prices. The *Financial Times* industrial ordinary share index, which stood at 339 when Mr Callaghan introduced his Budget in 1965, reached 521·9 in September 1968. It cannot have been the intention of the Chancellor, or of Professor Kaldor, to engineer a fifty per cent rise in share prices.

It seems likely, then, that the tax 'reforms' of 1965 have not only failed to achieve what their sponsors hoped, but have had some side-effects they may well not have welcomed. Other side effects include an enormous rise in the complexity of tax collection. On the Government side, the main effect has been obvious overloading of the Inland Revenue, despite massive staff increases. For industry the main effects have been more frequent and more expensive recourse to professional advice and an increase in unproductive record-keeping, frequently coupled with damaging uncertainties about the size and incidence of the tax burden.

The failure of the 1965 tax changes to achieve their intended effects on capital investment, applies equally to the new system of investment grants which was introduced in 1966. To quote *The Times*:* *Corporate investment incentives also await new thinking. The voice of the Board of Trade has been heard in the land admitting that the Investment Grant system 'needs review'. This is the standard euphemism for 'has been a failure'.*

This sad record in capital investment perhaps explodes once and for all the theory that governments can manipulate the tax system in such a way that industry will go on investing in face of a whole battery of policies which in total discourage enterprise. In Chapter 12 we suggest that industrial investment could not conceivably be expected to grow in face of a continuous procession of deflationary tax increases and credit restrictions, with threats of price control added to the limitations on profit earning. Against such a background Mr Callaghan's 'reforms' were at best irrelevant.

In fact, if they are allowed to continue they are likely to have long term harmful effects. The rush of 'easy' mergers, some of them quite clearly ill considered in industrial terms, is itself likely to do economic damage. More long term damage, however, is likely to arise from the penalisation of the shareholder through double taxation and the attempt to separate his interests from those of his company. An economy in which capital investment has been depressingly low for two decades is surely not the place in which to practise maximum discouragement of those able and willing to supply funds for industrial expansion. The most constructive critics of our taxation system are now, ironically enough, urging a return to essentially the company taxation system which existed before Mr Callaghan's 'reforms', or at least to a system of corporation tax which does not feverishly discriminate against dividend distribution.

* *The Times*, 9 April 1969.

EFFECTS OF SELECTIVE EMPLOYMENT TAX

The theoretical justifications which accompanied the introduction of the Selective Employment Tax in 1966 are now rarely heard. Claims that it would accelerate economic growth by enforcing the transfer of labour from service industries to manufacturing, for example, have disappeared into limbo, if only for the reason that unemployment in manufacturing industry has been running at near-record post-war levels since the end of 1966. There were, in fact, some modest reductions in the numbers employed in certain groups of service industries between June 1966 and June 1967. Those affected included the distributive trades and catering, but the financial and professional services group increased its employment over the same period. It is difficult to estimate how far the modest fall in employment in the service industries has been due to SET and how far it has resulted from the general deflationary situation and from increases in productivity. What seems certain is that any effect of the tax in bringing about a shift in employment patterns has been minute in scale.

It also seems certain that the tax has proved a successful instrument in raising more revenue in an already highly taxed economy. It has also had a major effect in raising prices—Mr Aubrey Jones, Chairman of the Prices and Incomes Board, has gone on record as suspecting that the tax has just one effect, higher prices.* One particular example is the effect on British hotels, where SET has pushed up prices by around five per cent, which has hardly benefited British tourism at a time when the prices of foreign package tours have been held steady. A further effect of SET has, of course, been the squeeze on company liquidity which has arisen from the 'forced loan' nature of the collection of the tax. It is reasonable to assume that the resources thus tied up would have produced greater economic benefit to the nation if left in the hands of industry.

The Conservative Party has pledged itself to abolish the Selective Employment Tax when it returns to power.†

EFFECTS ON SMALL COMPANIES

From the 1965 Budget onwards claims have been persistently and often vociferously made that the Government's fiscal and monetary policies were causing especial hardship to small companies in Britain. Apart from the notorious close company provisions, the change to investment grants had worked to the disadvantage of small companies. The continuous and usually intensifying credit squeezes characteristic of Labour's term of office had much more serious effects upon small companies than upon their larger brethren.

* *Evening Standard*, 3 March 1969.
† *Make Life Better*, Conservative Party, 1968.

Confiscatory measures such as the special charge on investment income imposed in the 1968 Budget, and the forced loans required under SET and the Imports Deposit Scheme also had disproportionately large effects on the small firm.

The difficulties of small companies were investigated during 1967 and 1968 by the Confederation of British Industry, and the report was published in September 1968.*

This report sensibly began by stressing the importance of small companies to the British economy: *The vast majority of corporate concerns in manufacturing industry in the UK consist of small firms; they are responsible for one-third of the total turnover and the output of many larger organisations is dependent upon the components which the small firms supply. If Britain's 80,000 small firms were to close down tomorrow, 2½ million workers would lose their jobs, over £6,000 million of industrial output would vanish and most of the larger firms would grind quickly and painfully to a halt.* The report also stressed that all the statistical evidence did not imply inefficiency on the part of small companies, but instead suggested that they tended to grow more rapidly and to be more profitable than larger concerns.

In considering *factors which may inhibit the growth of small firms* the CBI Report made the following points:

Much legislation seems to be directed against small companies; the provisions of the Finance Act 1965 dealing with close companies have borne particularly heavily on small firms, very many of which are close companies.† They have lost confidence in the future, and are therefore reluctant to invest more money for the expansion of their businesses. Furthermore any general recession in business affects small firms severely, particularly where their output is dependent on that of their large customers. This dependence frequently leads them to concentrate on a limited range of products and they lack the resources to enable them to diversify sufficiently to counteract the effects of a recession on the part of their large customers. Limitations on credit are more injurious to small than large firms, partly because they suffer particularly from any delay in receiving payment from their customers and partly because their resources make it difficult for them to weather the storm of a recession.

Legislation and regulations by the Government on employment and conditions of work are also felt to be detrimental to small firms' growth. Whilst small firms appreciate the social purpose behind such legislation, it imposes burdens upon them which are less easy to bear than for large companies. For instance, National Insurance, redundancy payments and Training Boards cause records to be kept,

* *Britain's Small Firms*, Confederation of British Industry, 1968.
† The 1969 Finance Act removed some elements of discrimination against close companies.

and extra clerical work to be done, which occupies the time of staff and sometimes even of directors, which could be spent more productively. The engagement of one more clerical assistant may easily increase the clerical staff of a small firm engaged on record keeping by one hundred per cent: a large firm which may have a hundred employees so occupied adds on one per cent to its complement by taking on an additional clerk to cope with the records required to comply with Government enactments. Such measures as these, although eminently desirable in themselves, all constitute a drain on the small firm's limited available capital.

The biggest factor in Government legislation to which small firms attribute their difficulties is the level of taxation, which leaves the firms insufficient capital to finance expansion of production or export. Many small firms contribute substantially to the export effort but much of this is necessarily indirect; they do not therefore benefit from any special assistance which may be made available to exporters as such. The provision of the Finance Acts in regard to remuneration of directors of close companies can mean valuable men cannot be adequately rewarded and they go elsewhere. In addition, the distribution of profits laid down by the Finance Act 1965 means that the amount of capital available for ploughing back into the firm is much less than is needed for a growing business. The burden of taxation is so high that many small firms are being driven out of business; even when they are able to survive, the rate of return which they can secure has now become so small, that the risks involved in expansion, especially in the export field, are frequently not considered to be worth taking, especially as estate duty reduces the incentive to build up a family business.

The small close company has suffered a further very serious blow in the 1968 Budget; this imposed a special charge on investment income. The shares of many small companies are held by members of the family, some of whom serve as the company's directors and draw their income from the business, partly as salary and partly in the form of dividends. The company is required to distribute sixty per cent of its profits; this is now to be subject retrospectively to the special charge, as a consequence of which the taxation imposed on the receipts from a small business may well be in excess of one hundred per cent. If the recipients have no other source of income, the tax can only be paid by disposing of some part of the assets of the company—assuming, of course, that a buyer can be found who is willing to pay a reasonable price for assets which are in effect the subject of a 'forced sale'. This imposition is likely to have a crucial effect on many small close companies.

In considering measures which might assist small companies the CBI enquiry observed: *The Government has, however, an important role to play. Tax changes to remove the disabilities imposed upon private firms are very necessary. At present the discrimination against family businesses is severe; the liability to income tax and surtax direction is unjust and damaging to the economy and the further burden created by the special charge on investment income is penal. Private businesses should be encouraged to plough back as much profit as they consider necessary for their expansion, not discouraged from so doing. Estate duty is almost equally damaging and would be even more so if ways had not been devised to overcome its most harmful effects. Nevertheless there have been many instances where small firms have been forced into liquidation in order to meet the estate duty payable on the death of the principal shareholder; others are likely to face a similar fate as a consequence of the special charge.*

Any change in taxation procedure that results in increased cash resources to small firms must be welcomed. Unfortunately the investment grant scheme has worked in exactly the opposite direction.

The fact that firms can now no longer aggregate their minor items of capital expenditure as they could under the old investment allowance system, means that the small firm has to keep far more detailed and costly records than would be commercially justified. Apart from this many of the items such as typewriters, office calculators and drawing boards, on which it could hitherto claim grant are now exempt with the result that the cash flow benefit is markedly less than under the old system; and half a carrot can never be as good an incentive as a whole carrot.

All this constitutes a formidable indictment of the effects of Government measures, and particularly of so-called tax 'reforms', on organisations responsible for one-third of Britain's industrial turnover.

EFFECTS OF A £14,000 MILLION TAX BURDEN

As we have seen, Labour increased taxes between October 1964 and December 1968 by £2,625 million; allowing for increasing yields due to largely inflationary increases in incomes and profits, Britain now carries a tax burden of over £14,000 million. It is difficult to see how anyone can expect British industry to prosper and expand while the whole community labours under the impact of a rapidly rising tax burden. The ultimate determinant of investment decisions is demand expectations, and so long as industry is faced with the spectacle of the British Chancellor of the Exchequer getting up at least twice a year to slap on several hundred million pounds of extra taxes these expectations are not likely to be pitched very high. Nobody who knows how investment decisions are taken in industry can have any doubt that the best way of stimulating a boom in capital investment would be to hold out the now unusual prospect of at least a period of stability in the tax burden, and preferably, of course, a reduction.

Within this framework one can easily pick some changes in the incidence of taxation which would be minute in their effects on a £14,000 million Budget, but could have substantial effects on industrial progress. The most obvious of these, and one which has been continuously canvassed for years is reduction in our fantastic top rates of surtax, which quite clearly make it impossible to reward top executives on anything like the scale enjoyed by those in other major industrial nations. Adjustment of this extraordinary international anomaly would make possible better rewards lower down the executive scale and remove from Britain the stigma of having the lowest paid management, in real terms, in the industrial world.

Restoration of the incentives inherent in stock options, which was so casually and foolishly destroyed in the Budgets of 1965 and 1966, would also allow British industry to offer its executives an incentive to enterprise and effort which has been found effective in the United States.

In its 1964 General Election Manifesto the Labour Party made the admirable promise: *the general effect of our tax changes will be to stimulate enterprise, not to penalise it.* Failure to live up to this sentiment must have contributed enormously to the shattering destruction of so many other hopes on which the Government set its heart.

CHAPTER TEN

The effects of Prices and Incomes Policy

Of all Labour's measures of intervention in industry, none has created more consistent controversy than Prices and Incomes Policy. For most of the period under review rarely a week has passed without some problem in this field making the headlines. It has been the subject of three Acts of Parliament, half a dozen White Papers, and one hundred reports by the National Board for Prices and Incomes; it has taken up an enormous amount of ministerial time and put a corresponding strain on management and officials in industry and the trade unions; it has caused a good deal of irritation to industrialists, and unlike most of the Government's other measures of intervention, has also irked and alienated many of Labour's traditional supporters in the trade union movement.

WHAT HAS BEEN ACHIEVED BY ALL THIS?

The prime objects of the Policy were to hold down earnings nationally to a level compatible with increases in productivity and keep the general level of prices stable. The tables on pages 97, 98 and 99 show respectively the course of earnings and prices in Britain since 1960. While the figures in these tables have been the subject of a number of distorting factors—notably, sweeping increases in taxation on the prices side and changes in working hours on the wages side—a comparison of the period 1960–64 in each table with the period 1964–68 suggests that the Policy has had little effect in achieving its avowed prime objects.

This superficial conclusion is confirmed by more refined studies. Professor Reddaway, for example,* surveying the prospects for a voluntary Policy in 1966 concluded that it would be *the height of folly to expect more than a very modest contribution from this machinery* and suggested that it would be a remarkable success if a voluntary system could reduce the rise of incomes and home costs by as much as one per cent at a given pressure of demand. A later study by Frank Blackaby and Michael Artis, in March 1968,† when

* *Lloyds Bank Review*, January 1966.
† *District Bank Review*, March 1968.

legislative sanctions had been given to the Policy, showed that the rise in average earnings during the twenty months from October 1964 to June 1966 was, if anything slightly *higher* than might have been expected. During the period from June 1966 to October 1967, which included the 'freeze' and 'period of severe restraint' average earnings rose just over five and a half per cent. Blackaby and Artis concluded that this was roughly what might have been expected from natural forces. They concluded: *so far, then, there does not appear to be a great deal to show for the effort that has been put into Incomes Policy.* Progress during 1968, which was not covered by the above authorities, does not indicate any greater effectiveness for the Policy in restraining earnings. They rose by seven per cent, on a seasonally adjusted basis, between December 1967 and October 1968, prompting a rise in consumers' expenditure which was one of the causes of the 'mini-budget' of November 1968.

This unmoderated rise in earnings would have done little damage to the economy if one of the other objects of the Prices and Incomes Policy, a substantial rise in productivity, had been achieved. The table on page 100 gives some indicators of the course of productivity increase in Britain since 1960. In crude terms it suggests that the rate of growth in productivity increase was marginally higher during the period 1964–68 than it was during the period 1960–64. The effect is not particularly pronounced, being the difference between an apparent fourteen and a half per cent growth over the earlier period, and sixteen per cent growth over the period 1964–68. The apparent rate of productivity increase following devaluation may be misleading, for it is well established that deceptively large productivity rises can be indicated at a period when slack in the economy is being rapidly taken up. Most expert opinion suggests that the underlying trend rate in productivity growth during 1968 was only around three and a half per cent per annum, which is roughly in line with what could be expected from projections of the established trend line during the 1960s. It can be safely concluded that the Prices and Incomes Policy had few, if any, discernible effects in pushing up productivity in Britain as it was operated between 1964 and 1968.

Minimal results in terms of moderating earnings increases or raising productivity could, in fact have been predicted from a study of experience in many European countries which had attempted to operate Incomes Policies since 1950. The Economic Commission for Europe, in a major study of such policies,* suggested that they *have not proved strikingly effective instruments of economic management. The policies have had achievements to record but they are limited and*

* *Incomes in Post-war Europe: a study of policies, growth and distribution*, Economic Commission for Europe, Geneva, 1967.

temporary achievements. What, in effect, the study showed was that in most European countries the maximum successes achieved by Incomes Policy had been to hold back earnings for a short period, which had been followed by an unusually sharp rise. In so far as there had been more lasting successes, extraneous factors such as high unemployment levels or mass immigration had been major factors.

Some economists would claim that only marginal results could possibly be predicted from economic theory for the operation of Incomes Policy in a market economy. The most famous exponent of this line of thought is Professor Frank Paish, who suggested in September 1964* that an Incomes Policy could not be effective at

COURSE OF WAGES AND EARNINGS SINCE 1960
Index numbers 1958 = 100

	Weekly wage rates	Hourly wage rates	Normal weekly hours	Weekly earnings	Hourly earnings	Hourly earnings	Average weekly hours
	In all Industries					In manufacturing	
1960	105·3	107·0	98·4	111·5	111·3	112·0	99·9
1961	109·7	113·9	96·3	118·3	118·9	119·6	98·5
1962	113·7	119·1	95·5	122·5	124·3	124·0	97·6
1963	117·8	123·5	95·4	127·5	129·3	128·8	97·5
1964	123·4	129·9	95·0	136·6	139·2	137·7	98·2
1965	128·7	138·0	93·3	146·7	152·3	149·0	97·0
1966	134·7	147·3	91·5	156·2	164·5	160·5	95·5
1967	139·6	153·1	91·2	161·4	170·2	167·1	94·8
1968	148·8	163·5	91·0				95·5
1967 I	136·8	149·8	91·3	156·1	—	163·2	94·1
II	138·0	151·2	91·3	161·1	167·6	166·3	94·9
III	140·6	154·2	91·1	162·9	—	167·5	95·2
IV	143·1	157·1	91·1	165·2	172·8	171·0	95·1
1968 I	146·7	161·2	91·0	170·2	—	178·2	94·5
II	148·0	162·7	91·0	173·8	180·1	179·1	96·1
III	149·1	163·8	91·0	175·1		179·2	96·0
IV	151·3	166·2	91·0				
September	149·6	164·4	91·0	175·9		180·3	95·7
October	150·0	164·8	91·0	177·4		181·0	95·9
November	151·0	165·9	91·0	179·7		184·5	95·9
December	152·9	168·0	91·0				96·1
1969 Jan.	154·3	169·5	91·0				

Seasonally adjusted.   *Source: NIESR.*

* *Policy for Incomes?*, F. W. Paish and Jossleyn Hennessy, Institute of Economic Affairs, 1964.

COURSE OF PRIC

	Capital goods					
	All assets	Plant, vehicles, etc.	Dwellings	Other building	Export unit values	R: pr
1957	97	97	99	97	101	9
1958	100	100	100	100	100	1C
1959	99	100	98	98	99	10
1960	100	100	99	98	101	10
1961	102	103	102	100	101	10
1962	105	105	106	105	102	1C
1963	107	105	110	108	105	11
1964	110	108	111	111	107	1
1965	114	113	116	114	109	12
1966	118	117	122	118	113	12
1967	120	118	123	120	115	12
1968					124	13
1966 III	119	119	123	118	114	12
IV	120	119	123	119	114	12
1967 I	120	119	122	119	115	12
II	119	118	123	120	115	12
III	120	118	123	120	116	12
IV	119	117	123	121	117	12
1968 I	120	119	124	121	122	13
II	123	122	126	123	124	13
III	124	123	127	123	126	13
IV					127	13
September					126	13
October					126	13
November					127	1:
December					127	13
1969 January						1

CE 1960   *Index numbers, 1958 = 100*

			Consumer goods and services					
al	Food	Drink, tobacco	Housing (inc. rent and rates)	Durable goods	Clothing	All other goods	Services	Total final prices
3	98·6	98·0	89·9	100·0	99·1	97·7	96·5	97·8
0	100·0	100·0	100·0	100·0	100·0	100·0	100·0	100·0
6	101·2	97·9	105·3	97·9	99·5	99·8	101·8	100·8
5	100·7	99·4	108·5	96·9	100·8	100·3	104·5	102·0
5	102·2	103·9	113·4	97·8	102·5	104·0	110·0	104·8
4	105·7	109·8	120·5	97·6	105·5	107·6	112·4	108·2
9	107·5	111·2	128·6	91·8	107·0	109·1	115·1	110·1
1	110·4	117·2	136·5	92·5	108·7	111·8	117·7	113·0
2	114·2	128·7	144·7	94·7	111·0	116·3	122·2	117·7
6	117·8	133·1	153·8	96·2	113·9	120·4	127·5	122·2
3	120·0	135·1	159·5	97·3	115·4	122·5	131·8	125·2
4	119·3	133·8	155·1	97·7	114·5	123·1	127·7	123·7
9	117·9	135·3	157·0	102·8	114·5	122·0	130·6	124·3
3	119·1	134·6	158·3	96·5	115·1	121·0	130·7	123·9
8	120·6	135·6	157·4	95·9	115·7	120·7	131·8	124·5
3	120·8	135·3	160·0	96·7	115·8	125·0	132·3	125·9
7	119·5	134·9	162·3	99·8	115·0	124·5	132·2	126·5
7	121·6	136·3	163·8	96·1	116·0	124·4	133·6	127·6
2	123·6	139·9	164·2	102·2	116·9	130·2	135·8	130·9
2	124·5	140·4	166·9	103·5	117·3	134·8	137·4	132·7

Source: NIESR

levels of unemployment below two per cent, while the rate of earnings increase would automatically be held in check at levels of unemployment above two and a quarter per cent.

EFFECTS ON PRICES

Between 1964 and the second quarter of 1968 total final prices rose by 15·6 per cent compared with a rise of 10·8 per cent between 1960 and 1964. The more often quoted index of retail prices rose by nineteen per cent between October 1964 and December 1968 compared with a rise of thirteen and a half per cent between 1960 and 1964. These figures evidently suggest the Prices and Incomes Policy had a negligible effect on prices, just as they make nonsense of Labour's 1964 manifesto promise* of a *plan for stable prices* and its 1966 claim† that the Government had *launched the first serious attack on the rising costs of living*.

In fact, there are a number of complicating factors. Between 1964 and the end of 1968 the Government raised indirect taxes on no fewer than five separate occasions, with consequent increases in

COURSE OF PRODUCTIVITY SINCE 1960

Index numbers, 1958 = 100, seasonally adjusted

	Output per person employed in							Output per man-hour worked in manu-facturing
	Gross domestic product	Total industrial production	Total manu-facturing	Metals, metal-using	Textiles	Mining	Con-struction	
1960	107	110	110	108	114	106	107	110
1961	108	110	109	106	111	109	110	110
1962	109	111	110	106	113	115	109	113
1963	113	116	116	111	121	119	110	119
1964	118	123	123	118	129	125	114	126
1965	120	125	126	120	133	126	113	130
1966	122	127	127	121	135	128	115	133
1967	125	130	130	121	140	133	125	137
1968		139	138	129	161	142		145
1967 I	124	128	128	120	136	132	121	137
II	125	130	129	121	138	134	124	136
III	126	130	129	120	139	133	126	136
IV	128	134	133	123	149	135	128	140
1968 I	130	136	136	125	158	139	127	144
II	129	137	137	127	162	140	131	144
III	131	139	138	129	161	142	133	144
IV		141	141	132	164	147		147
September		139	138	129	162	142		144
October		140	140	130	160	143		146
November		141	142	133	164	145		148
December		142	141	132	166	152		147

Source: NIESR

* Labour Party General Election Manifesto, 1964.
† Labour Party General Election Manifesto, 1966.

many prices. It also introduced and then increased the Selective Employment Tax, which generated price rises over a very wide range of goods. The situation has been further complicated by a twenty-five and a half per cent increase in the prices charged by nationalised industries, which are basic to most industrial operations. What happened between October 1964 and the end of 1968 was that the private sector of industry achieved considerable success in keeping its prices stable in face of sharply rising costs, including increased raw material costs following devaluation. Prices of manufactured goods rose by 14·3 per cent between the end of 1964 and October 1968, with the major part of the increase coming after devaluation in November 1967.

Obviously Prices and Incomes Policy was only one of many factors influencing private sector prices. It is very difficult to separate this influence from others such as competition and demand levels, but there is a certain amount of presumptive evidence that the Policy had somewhat more influence on private sector prices than on wages during the period under study. Certain politically sensitive prices such as those of bread and beer were certainly held back for quite prolonged periods by Prices Policy measures. Much of the evidence for more effectiveness on the prices side of the Policy is more subjective, deriving mainly from statements from a fairly high proportion of industrialists that they felt constrained by the Policy and tended to defer price increases which they would otherwise have judged necessary, whether or not they were subject to formal control. The effects in statistical terms may well have been quite small, but Prices Policy seems to have enjoyed at least a modest measure of success in creating 'a climate of opinion' which helped to slow the advance in prices.

If, in fact, Prices and Incomes Policy achieved more success in moderating price increases than incomes increases, it would be difficult to claim this as a successful outcome in general economic terms. One of the main aims of economic management over the period has been to restrain the growth of consumers' expenditure. Obviously, allowing earnings to rise faster than prices encourages such expenditure instead of depressing it.

A further disadvantage of continuing disproportion between earnings increases and prices increases has been pointed out by commentators such as Blackaby and Artis. What, in effect, the disproportion tends to achieve is a lower level of manufacturers' profit with consequent depression of investment levels.

INCIDENTAL BENEFITS

On the statistical evidence, it is, perhaps, not too sweeping to sum up Prices and Incomes Policy during the period 1964–68 as near failure.

There are supporters of the Policy who would accept this statistical verdict, but nevertheless claim that the Policy has been successful or useful in bringing some incidental benefits. The benefits usually enumerated are in effect, the propaganda effects which the Policy may have achieved over its period of operation.

The major claim in this area is that the reports of the National Board for Prices and Incomes, and Government interventions preceding and following such reports, have reduced the importance of inflationary elements like 'cost of living' and 'comparability' in wage bargaining and substituted important factors such as productivity and what the national interest can afford.

It seems undeniable that some effects of this sort have occurred. Taking two of the major wage issues in 1968, for example, the railway pay issue was resolved on the basis of undertakings by the railway unions to conclude rapidly a productivity agreement; the dispute over engineering wages was eventually resolved on the basis of substantial increases in basic rates, but it was notable that the Engineering Employers Federation adhered strongly to the principle that future rises in engineering wages should be geared to locally bargained productivity agreements. Many proposed trade union wages claims have been turned down by the TUC's vetting machinery as being inconsistent with the national interest, as defined either by incomes policy criteria or Congress' own standards; in a proportion of cases, at least the claims have either been moderated or deferred. It is also the case that the existence of incomes policy criteria has stiffened the resolve of many employers in wage negotiations, so that in at least some cases unions may have been influenced into more moderate settlements or the conclusion of productivity agreements which they would otherwise not have considered.

In principle, such results are bound to be beneficial to the economy. Their long term influence may well be more important than what has been achieved to date, for many of the so-called productivity based rises which have been given have owed more to chance improvements of productivity or to expressions of vague intention than to genuine concessions by employees to remove restrictions on efficient working.

On the prices side, the propaganda influences of the Policy have not been particularly clear or consistent. The most probable beneficial influence in the NBPI's reports on price questions have been continuing emphasis on productive and distributive efficiency, usually backed by some practical and sometimes provocative suggestions for achieving these ends. This apart, it is difficult to isolate any major potential influences from the mass of reports produced by the Board or from the Government's actions in support of the Policy. The net effect can perhaps be summed up as constituting a minor encouragement to industry to seek improvement of efficiency as a means of making price rises unnecessary, but it is difficult to believe that normal competitive forces do not already act much more powerfully to the same end.

WAS IT WORTH IT?

Even if one concedes substantial propaganda value, one must inevitably ask, bearing in mind its very modest beneficial practical effects, whether the massive effort which has gone into Prices and Incomes Policy has been worthwhile.

A well-known Left wing critic of Incomes Policy, Mr Eric Heffer, MP, said at the end of 1968* that he did not support the Policy because it only produced a one per cent result, *and one per cent isn't worth splitting the British Labour Movement down the middle.* This was, of course, a partisan point of view, but if one translates it into national terms it raises an issue of great importance. Given its admittedly modest effects, is the attempt to operate a Prices and Incomes Policy worth all the controversy, effort, bureaucracy, and restrictiveness it involves?

In these terms, the cost of the Policy is undoubtedly high. Apart from the efforts required from the National Board for Prices and Incomes, the Policy is a substantial user of civil servants' time in half a dozen ministries; this bureaucratic effort calls forth a still greater effort from industry, imposing substantial involvement in operating the early warning system, and in the time of top management both in relating business decisions to the Policy requirements or participating in investigations when they are ordered. The delays involved in awaiting ministerial decisions or Board reports, add yet another element of uncertainty to business management.

The almost continuous controversy surrounding the Policy, or the details of its operation, are another element of cost. In this atmosphere both industrialists and trade unionists are quick to perceive anomalies and to feel that they are being unfairly treated—particularly as specifically political considerations often appear to influence the operation of the Policy. Examples here include the way in which the Policy has from time to time apparently been 'stretched' to accommodate the demands of unions with power to disrupt the national economy, and the way in which politically sensitive prices (i.e. those where price increases are supposed to influence votes) have been singled out by especially vigorous attempts at restraint. Similarly, price increases in the nationalised industries (of muc larger dimensions than those usually sought by the private sector) were approved on the somewhat curious grounds that they were

* 'The Money Programme', BBC Television, December 1968.

necessary if these industries were to achieve the targets set for them by the Government. The sense of unfairness left by the operation of a policy containing many apparent anomalies can hardly be beneficial to the national economy.

Relatively few people seem to care very passionately about erosions of personal freedom nowadays, but it should be observed that the Prices and Incomes Policy has in fact placed substantial restrictions on liberties that were hitherto taken for granted in Britain. The most notable of these now-restricted liberties are those of employer and employee representatives to implement wage bargains freely arrived at, and the erstwhile right of the businessman to ask whatever prices he deems most profitable without having to seek anyone's permission. In addition, legislation in support of the Prices and Incomes Policy creates a number of new offences, including that of failing to give information to the Prices and Incomes Board when required.

LONG TERM EFFECTS

These are immediate and obvious effects of Prices and Incomes Policy, but it is also important to pin-point damaging long term effects, which may arise if it is accepted as continuing in operation indefinitely. One area in which the perpetuation of what is essentially a rather crude and erratic form of price control is likely to cause damage is capital investment. Every appraisal of an investment must inevitably be based on price assumptions, and no investment is likely to be regarded as attractive unless the industrialist can be reasonably certain of being able to achieve gross margins which will fully cover his costs and provide adequate profit. It is reasonable to suppose that in fields where industrialists suspect that prices might be artificially held down, adequate investment may not in future be forthcoming. If this does not happen, what certainly seems likely is the avoidance of the riskier forms of investment in such areas, and this is usually precisely the most technically advanced type of development which Britain badly needs.

On the wages side some damaging long term effects could flow from the fact that Incomes Policy substantially seeks to distort or modify market forces. While these forces have not necessarily always worked to produce the most immediately beneficial economic results, they have tended in over-all terms to produce desirable effects, such as labour mobility from declining industries to growth industries and a pattern of differential rewards for differing skills and responsibilities. Similarly, the market system has given companies wishing to increase their recruiting attractions or the stability of their labour forces plenty of elbow room for achieving such things through appropriate payment systems. No doubt such considerations are taken into account by the National Board for Prices and Incomes and the Department of Employment and Productivity, but the over-all effect of Incomes Policy is to impose rigidities on payment levels and differentials which could in the long term reduce mobility and incentive among the working population.

This is particularly the case because Incomes Policy has always included social objectives, such as the improvement of the lot of the lower paid, among its aims. Nobody would quarrel on humanitarian grounds with such objectives, but it is questionable whether the practice of permitting wage increases to the lowest paid and seeking to hold back advances for those with higher earnings is of long term economic benefit to the nation. Its obvious effect is to reduce differentials for skill and responsibility and thus to reduce the incentive to acquire extra skill or accept more onerous work. This must surely be the opposite of what the national economy needs.

A further general disincentive effect arises from the fact that, at least as so far applied, Incomes Policy is essentially a restrictive device. Its avowed object over the whole period under study has been to hold down the general level of incomes and personal living standards. This, of course, has been a perfectly logical objective in the economic circumstances of the time, but its inevitable consequence must be a dispiriting climate of opinion in which the prospective rewards for extra effort look disproportionately low. Whatever disincentive effects result from Incomes Policy have, of course, been enormously enhanced by increased taxation.

Enthusiasts for Incomes Policy will doubtless argue that it need not always be a restrictive device. Given a more expansive economic climate or a situation in which productivity was keeping pace with the general rise in incomes, the Policy could be used to provide more equitable distribution of 'the cake' among the numerous claimants. Some such intention was doubtless sincerely intended when Incomes Policy was sold to the Trades Union Congress in 1964 under the euphemism 'planned growth of incomes'. What is questionable about this concept is whether the ministrations of the National Board for Prices and Incomes and the Department of Employment and Productivity would in fact produce more satisfactory results in equity than the interplay of market forces and free bargaining. The climate of opinion within the trade union movement about the operation of Incomes Policy to date hardly supports the thesis that the authorities in Britain are especially well placed to devise wages systems that the working population recognises as being more satisfactory than those which would otherwise have been arrived at. Nor, indeed, does experience of governments as employers—of all political persuasions and in all countries—give any confidence that there is some practicable ideal wage system which can be arrived at if only enlightened central authority takes a hand.

SOME CONCLUSIONS

Writing in January 1969, the future of Prices and Incomes Policy looks to be in considerable doubt. The Labour Government is faced with difficult decisions on whether or not to take further legal sanctions when those in the Prices and Incomes Act 1968 expire at the end of the year. There is considerable dissension within the Labour Party, and probably within the Government, about the continuance of legal sanctions. The Conservative Party has not made its intentions on Prices and Incomes Policy clear, though on 28 January 1968, the 'shadow' Chancellor of the Exchequer hinted that the Prices and Incomes Board would not last long if the Conservatives came to power.

On objective evaluation, it is difficult to believe that the practical beneficial effects of a Government-operated Prices and Incomes Policy will ever outweigh its numerous disadvantages, or justify the rather frenetic efforts its operation involves. It is generally accepted in politics that some policies that are manifestly desirable in intention are unworkable in practice because they involve detailed intervention, anomaly, and discontent, quite disproportionate to their prospective benefits. Prices and Incomes Policy seems to be a case in point.

If this is accepted, then what is required is a gradual run-down of State intervention in this field. The relatively restrictive lower limits for 'early warning' notification should be widened. The Government should discipline itself to reduce the number of references to the National Board for Prices and Incomes, confining itself to a few crucial issues where it believes the national interest or some major point of principle to be manifestly at stake. The legal sanctions should be allowed to lapse and the temptation to restore them whenever some crisis looms should be resisted. Following these principles would remove the 'over-government' element which has not only made the Policy a bureaucratic institution but has caused much of the irritation felt by both industrialists and trade unionists. Given a substantial decrease in its detailed involvement in Prices and Incomes questions, it would be appropriate for the Government to step up the extent to which it uses its considerable persuasive powers in those issues which it deems to be of manifest national importance. This would appear to be an appropriate modification of the Prices and Incomes Policy for a Labour Government, involving an acknowledgment of the disadvantages of over-detailed intervention without sacrificing what it may well regard as the essential principle of giving

Government a continuing influence in wage and prices movements.

If a Conservative administration succeeds the present one, it is reasonable to assume, and indeed to hope for, a considerable restoration of incentives and market forces. In such circumstances the main and perhaps the only sanctions against unwarranted incomes or prices increases would be competitive forces, which would similarly provide the incentive to increase productivity. A moderate Conservative Government, might, in fact, on mature consideration find it useful to have some institution available to pronounce on occasional key issues where it was felt that some kind of objective statement of what appeared to be the national interest was desirable. The existing Prices and Incomes Board, appropriately redirected, might fulfil this role, though one would expect it to be very sparingly used. Under such a regime, of course, there would be no legislative backing for any influence the Government felt itself obliged to try to exert on incomes or prices questions.

The Prices and Incomes Policy, as devised and operated by Labour over the period 1964-68 must be regarded as a well-intentioned experiment which failed. It failed in part because of the acknowledged and inherent difficulties of operating such a policy in a market economy. It also failed, perhaps, because it operated on a basis of over-fussy and unduly detailed intervention into wide areas of industrial and trade union concern and produced the exasperated psychological reactions which seem to be inevitably associated with detailed State involvement. There is surely a lesson here when other schemes of State intervention, however seemingly desirable to the theoreticians, are being devised.

CHAPTER ELEVEN

The effects of regional policies

Although the motivations behind regional policy are primarily social and political, a persuasive economic case can also be argued for State intervention to redress the imbalance in regional prosperity and economic growth which has existed and intensified in Britain since the early part of this century.

The essence of this case is that the less prosperous regions, with their characteristics of unemployment levels well above the national average, constitute a pool of under-used resources. Fuller use of these resources should permit faster national economic growth without the inflationary pressures (excessive unfilled vacancies, wage drift, etc.) generated by growth in the more prosperous regions. In addition, diversion of economic growth to areas of relatively low economic activity has the advantage of avoiding further increases in congestion in the prosperous regions, with their related economic and amenity costs.

Against the expected benefits of correction of regional imbalance must be set the costs of intervention. Some of these are direct and measurable, as in the case of financial inducements given to companies to persuade them to set up or extend operations in regions of low prosperity. Others are indirect and extremely difficult to quantify. Within this category come the costs of economic distortions and inefficiencies which may be caused by measures of intervention, which are either ill-conceived or have uncovenanted side effects. Further costs, also difficult to detect and measure, are likely to arise from mistakes in the administration of schemes which allow substantial discretion to the authorities.

The purpose of this chapter is to evaluate the achievements of regional policy between 1964 and 1968 and its costs and its side effects. An attempt is made thereafter to determine to what extent state intervention in the regional distribution of industry appears to be justified by its results and to suggest modifications in policy or practice which might improve the results, either by increasing effectiveness or reducing direct or indirect costs.

EFFECTS ON EMPLOYMENT

Since the principal social and political aim of regional policy is to reduce disparities in unemployment levels between regions, the most obvious indicator of the working of interventionist measures is the regional unemployment statistics.

The table below summarises the relationships between unemployment in the present development areas, the non-development areas and Great Britain as a whole since 1959. The table on pages 110 and 111 shows regional unemployment statistics in detail during the period.

These tables suggest that regional policies are achieving some success in reducing disparities in unemployment rates. Between 1959 and 1966 average unemployment rates in the development areas were consistently at least double the national average. In 1967 and 1968 the development area averages fell respectively to 188 per cent and 170 per cent of the national average. Comparing the peak unemployment years of 1963 and 1967, two of the development areas, Scotland and the North, achieved a substantial improvement in 1967. In 1963 Scotland's average unemployment rose to 4·8 per cent of the working population; in 1967 it averaged 3·9 per cent. Similarly, unemployment in the North rose to five per cent in 1963, but in 1967 it averaged four per cent of the working population of the region.

It can, in fact, be argued that the unemployment figures for the development regions understate the achievements of regional policy in evening out the spread of unemployment. There has been an

UNEMPLOYMENT RATES (wholly unemployed) 1959–67
Annual Averages—percentages

	Great Britain (1)	Development Areas (2)	Rest of Great Britain (3)	Difference between Development Areas and rest of Great Britain (2)–(3)
1959	2·0	3·8	1·6	2·2
1960	1·5	3·2	1·1	2·1
1961	1·3	2·8	0·9	1·9
1962	1·8	3·6	1·3	2·3
1963	2·2	4·4	1·6	2·8
1964	1·6	3·5	1·1	2·4
1965	1·3	2·8	0·9	1·9
1966	1·4	2·7	1·1	1·6
1967	2·2	3·9	1·8	2·1

acceleration in the rate of run-down of coal mining and other traditional industries during the years 1965–68, particularly affecting the development regions Scotland, the North and Wales. Thus in the absence of effective measures to provide additional employment in these regions, significant increases in unemployment rates could have been expected instead of the falls which occurred.

The experience of Scotland and the North also gives some indication of the time-scale and cumulative nature of the effects of regional policy. Substantial parts of these two regions were the subject of measures to increase employment during the Conservative administration of 1959–64, mostly within the framework of the Local Employment Acts of 1960 and 1963. Wales did not receive so much attention, and a large part of South Wales was in fact descheduled from development area status in 1961, and not restored until 1965 when Labour was in office. It can reasonably be argued that the experience of Wales, where unemployment was 3·6 per cent in the 1963 recession, but 4·1 per cent in 1967, compares unfavourably with that of Scotland and the North because regional policy has not yet had time to work to full effect in Wales.

INDUSTRIAL BUILDING

One of the essential elements of the Government's regional policy is the attempt to force or persuade industrialists to site new or expansion projects in the development areas. Coercion comes via the issue (or refusal) of industrial development certificates; the premium on SET, the Regional Employment Premium, the various

UNEMPLOYME

		1960		1961		1962
		No. 000's	% of w/p	No. 000's	% of w/p	No. 000's
London & South-eastern	..	52·6	—	54·3	—	72·7
Eastern & Southern	.. ..	28·6	—	28·1	—	35·5
South-western	.. ..	20·6	1·7	17·8	1·4	22·5
West Midlands ..	.. ..	21·4	1·0	31·4	1·4	40·5
East Midlands ..	.. ..	13·1	—	13·0	—	17·9
Yorks & Humberside	.. ..	24·5	—	21·0	—	34·3
North-western	.. ..	57·8	1·9	49·3	1·6	76·8
Northern	.. ..	37·2	2·9	32·4	2·5	49·3
Wales	.. ..	26·0	2·7	24·9	2·6	30·7
Scotland ..	.. ..	78·7	3·6	68·4	3·1	83·1
Totals ..	.. ..	360·4	1·6	340·7	1·5	463·2

w/p = working population.
Figures given are monthly averages.

grants and loans available under the Local Employments Acts and the immediate availability at subsidised rents of 'advance' factories constitute the inducements. Obviously, if all these measures are working as expected, there should be a significant rise in the proportion of the nation's industrial building taking place within the development areas.

The table below shows what has occurred since 1960. It confirms that, comparing the period 1960–64 with 1965–67, the

INDUSTRIAL BUILDING IN THE DEVELOPMENT AREAS AS A % OF TOTAL INDUSTRIAL BUILDING IN GREAT BRITAIN

North	1960–1964	9·27%	1965–1967	8·43%
Wales	1960–1964	5·37%	1965–1967	9·73%
South-west	1960–1964	6·47%	1965–1967	5·76%
Scotland	1960–1964	9·68%	1965–1967	13·49%

Source: Central Statistical Office

proportion of total industrial building occurring in the development regions has risen from 30·8 per cent to 37·4 per cent. The table on page 112, showing floor areas approved under the IDC scheme during each year, suggests that the improvement in the development regions' share of total industrial building will continue during 1969 and 1970, when the 'approvals' become 'completions'. There are obvious links between industrial building and employment. Applicants for assistance under the Local Employment Acts and the Industrial Development Act are, in fact, required to estimate the

ONAL FIGURES

	1963		1964		1965		1966		1967	
s	% of w/p	No. 000's	% of w/p	No. 000's	% of w/p	No. 000's	% of w/p	No. 000's	% of w/p
7	—	57·4	—	50·5	0·9	54·9	0·9	93·3	1·6
7	—	28·5	—	26·8	1·0	34·0	1·2	51·4	1·8
9	2·1	20·5	1·5	20·9	1·6	24·5	1·8	33·8	2·5
9	2·0	21·6	0·9	20·4	0·9	31·7	1·3	57·8	2·5
7	—	13·6	—	13·3	0·9	15·8	1·1	26·0	1·8
5	—	26·4	—	22·8	1·1	25·4	1·2	44·4	2·1
6	3·1	62·5	2·1	48·4	1·6	45·5	1·5	74·9	2·9
4	5·0	44·0	3·3	34·3	2·6	35·1	2·6	53·1	4·0
0	3·6	25·7	2·6	25·9	2·6	29·4	2·9	40·3	4·1
8	4·8	80·3	3·6	65·5	3·0	63·5	2·9	84·6	3·9
2	2·5	380·6	1·6	328·8	1·4	359·7	1·5	559·5	2·4

Source: DEP

number of new jobs their building projects will create. While the changes in development area boundaries since 1965 make comparisons difficult, one estimate suggests that the number of new jobs created through building approvals in the development areas has been risen from 38,000 annually in 1960–64 to 86,000 annually in 1966–67.

CONTRIBUTION TO NATIONAL ECONOMIC GROWTH

From the foregoing it can be argued that a higher proportion of national economic growth has gone into the development regions during the period 1964–68 than would have occurred if the Government's successive measures of regional policy had not been adopted. It is much more difficult to argue that regional policy produced national economic growth which would otherwise not have occurred. What, at best, happened was that a certain amount of growth was diverted from the more prosperous regions to the development regions. Conceivably some growth which might have occurred in the prosperous regions was lost because of regional policies (see pp. 117 and 119).

The economic argument that the Government's regional policy would permit national economic growth without economic 'over-heating' remains not proven by the events of 1964–68. The rate of national economic growth, whether measured by the Gross National

INDUSTRIAL BUILDING IN GREAT BRITAIN*
New Standard Regions
Area approved during year†   Million square feet

	1960	1961	1962	1963	1964	1965	1966 a	1966 b	1967 a	1967 b
Great Britain ..	99·2	56·5	37·3	39·1	59·0	61·9	69·4	76·0	59·9	87·2
North	4·2	6·5	3·0	4·2	8·2	6·2	8·2	8·2	7·5	7·5
Yorkshire and Humberside ..	10·2	4·2	2·4	3·7	6·0	6·2	6·7	7·4	4·5	8·7
East Midlands ..	5·2	3·5	2·2	2·5	3·7	3·4	4·4	4·9	3·8	6·4
East Anglia ..	2·7	1·8	1·8	1·5	2·5	1·9	3·8	4·1	2·2	3·6
South-east ..	26·7	18·1	11·8	9·4	11·9	11·3	10·8	13·3	11·0	20·6
of which Greater London Council area	8·7	5·6	3·8	2·5	3·6	3·5	3·9	5·2	3·7	7·2
South-west ..	6·2	2·8	2·4	2·4	4·4	3·1	3·5	4·1	3·4	6·3
Wales	5·7	2·5	2·1	1·6	3·2	4·5	9·3	9·3	5·7	5·7
West Midlands ..	10·9	5·0	3·7	3·5	5·0	5·0	5·8	6·4	4·1	7·1
North-west ..	19·5	7·4	4·4	5·3	8·2	9·2	8·7	10·2	7·6	11·2
Scotland	7·7	4·9	3·7	5·0	5·9	11·0	8·2	8·2	10·2	10·2

* The figures relate to schemes over 5,000 square feet. The definition of industrial floor space was changed in all regions except North, Scotland and Wales in 1960–61. The ancillary space for storage, canteens, etc., excluded at that time has been included in the area of Industrial Development Certificates issued since mid-August 1966. The figures in column a for 1966 are estimates of the area which would have been approved on the 1960–61 to 1965 basis. The impact of this change cannot be related to completions.

† For all projects (new buildings, extensions to existing premises and buildings converted to industrial use) for which Industrial Development Certificates were issued.

Source: Abstract of Regional Statistics No. 4, 1968.

Product or the Index of Production, or by manufacturing investment was never comparable with that achieved in earlier peak periods. Thus tapping under-used regional resources to permit faster growth than had been achieved by the previous administration had little economic significance. What in fact occurred were periods of overheating without significant economic growth. Although this constituted a major failure in general economic policy, there is insufficient evidence to determine whether regional policy contributed to this failure or maybe prevented it from being worse.

COST OF REGIONAL POLICIES

Effectively, all that can legitimately be claimed for the Government's regional policies is that they have effected a modest reduction in unemployment rates in the development regions (particularly in Scotland and the North) and diverted a proportion of national economic growth away from the prosperous and overcrowded regions. Neither effect is particularly pronounced. The *National Institute Economic Review** summed up the 1964–67 employment figures as *tentative evidence that government regional policies may have been having some effect.*

This is not really very high praise. The Government's regional policies are now costing some £250 million† a year in public funds. This is nearly double the figure for 1967–68 and eight times public expenditure in 1964–65. Over the period 1965 to 1968 inclusive at least £500 million was spent on development area policies. It would constitute the most ignominious failure if these huge expenditures produced no discernible effects at all.

In fact, experience in other countries with location policies based on substantial loans and grants from public funds and major tax inducements shows that regional unemployment can be favourably affected if the total help is big enough. An OECD study of Scandinavian experience,‡ for example, concluded that *while it can be expected that this policy will have big effects on employment, the risk of making mistakes and using funds wrongly is undoubtedly high.*

The British Government's measures have so far produced useful rather than big effects on employment disparities between regions. Have there also been mistakes and wrong use of funds? To arrive at a sensible answer to this question, one must consider the side effects, indirect costs of regional policies, as well as attempting some kind of cost-benefit analysis of their acknowledged direct costs.

* *National Institute Economic Review*, February 1968.
† Mr Peter Shore gave these figures to the Regional Studies Association, 26 April 1968.
‡ *Active Manpower Policy, Scandinavian Regional Seminar, Final Report* OECD, Paris, 1967.

SIDE EFFECTS OF REGIONAL POLICIES

A number of studies and commentators have reported in varying degrees of detail on the side effects of Government measures designed to affect the location of industry in favour of the development areas. Some of these side effects arise directly from the whole 'package' of Government measures, while others arise directly from individual measures.

The most important side effects of the whole 'package' of measures can be summarised as follows:

Anomalies between areas. The development area system inevitably raises acute problems in the drawing of boundaries and major anomalies between competing companies. The difficulties of boundary drawing and deciding what areas should or should not be favoured with the generous package of regional policy measures have led to major discussion of the problems of the 'grey' areas and the appointment of the Hunt Committee.

At the same time, the steady advance in the benefits available to companies in the development areas has led to changes in the competitive situation between companies which do not necessarily make for industrial efficiency. Professor T. Wilson* has estimated that the combined effect of Government measures may amount to an average five per cent net subsidy on total costs to profitable firms following active investment policies in the development areas. The distribution of such significant assistance, irrespective of efficiency or of any factor other than location, can handicap the progress of efficient companies outside the development areas.

Rationalisation. One of the obvious effects of the assistance available in the development areas is that it can turn the otherwise unviable industrial unit into one which makes a modest profit. This may well be desirable on grounds of provision of employment, but it is a dubious contribution to national industrial efficiency. The CBI Regional Study,† considering the investment grants, reported: *they can encourage the establishment of projects which really waste capital and they can assist the re-equipment of unprofitable established units, which, despite re-equipment remain unprofitable and should be closed down. Investment grants prolong the life of the latter without justification.*

These strictures, in fact, apply to all the inducements offered in

* *Three Banks Review*, September 1967. 'Finance for Regional Industrial Development', T. Wilson.
† CBI Regional Study, *Regional development and distribution of industry policy*, September 1968.

support of regional policy. Between them they enable high-cost producers to survive, so long as they are sited in development areas. There is an inevitable conflict in this with another major aspect of Government policy, the drive to achieve rationalisation.

In terms of straight economic benefits to the nation, overcapacity situations should be resolved by the least efficient units going out of business. In industries where excess, inefficient capacity exists in the development areas, Government regional policy will thwart this aim. Artificial survival of inefficient units has the important side effect of causing undercapacity working of more efficient plant, and thus reducing the return on recent investment and discouraging further investment.

Mobility of labour. The Government's regional policies are essentially geared to the concept of taking jobs to people, rather than encouraging people to move to areas where vacancies urgently need filling. Other Government policies work in the opposite direction, encouraging geographical mobility of labour by devices like resettlement grants and part payments of removal expenses.

There is nothing inherently wrong in this apparent conflict of policies, for a dynamic economy requires both labour mobility and some relocation of industry. What can reasonably be questioned is the balance between the overwhelming resources provided to encourage relocation and the extremely modest inducements attached to labour mobility. Both the CBI Regional Study and the Brookings Report* have especially criticised the deterrents to labour mobility inherent in the Government's housing policies, while the National Board for Prices and Incomes† has recommended economic rents for council housing on a replacement-cost basis in place of the subsidised rents which tend to tie large sections of the population to particular locations.

Labour mobility is essential to the economy if growth and export-orientated industries are to prosper and the social problems caused by declining industries are to be solved. It is probably a fair criticism of the Government's regional policies that they provide too great a disincentive to labour mobility.

Discrimination against service industries. The Government's general policy of discrimination against service industries is carried over into all its regional policy measures. The regional employment premium

---

* *Britain's Economic Prospect*, Richard E. Caves and associates, The Brookngs Institution (Washington) and George Allen and Unwin Ltd (London).
† National Board for Prices and Incomes, *Increases in Rents of Local Authority Housing*.

is not payable to employers in the service industries; grants and loans under the Local Employment Acts are available to service industry employers only for projects which will provide more than fifty new jobs. As elsewhere, service industries in the development areas bear the full rigour of the Selective Employment Tax and are ineligible for investment grants. The net effect is that the disparity between manufacturing and service employers is even more marked in the development areas than in the rest of the country.

If discrimination against service industries is generally hard to justify (see Chapter 9) it seems especially indefensible in the development areas. As the CBI has pointed out, manufacturing industry cannot develop in these areas without corresponding growth of service industries. The penalties imposed on services increase manufacturers' distribution costs, which the CBI has characterised as an undesirable result in the development areas which are handicapped by their distance from the main centres of the population.

In its eagerness to limit the expansion of the service industries, the Government is jeopardising the regional policies to which it devotes such substantial resources.

Change and uncertainty. Between January 1960 and December 1967, six major sets of changes in regional policy measures were made. Seven Acts of Parliament substantially affecting industry's fortunes in the less prosperous regions were passed. The boundaries of areas entitled to receive special assistance were changed four times, and administrative policies and practices were radically altered on five occasions.

It is not surprising that industrialists operating in the less prosperous regions, or contemplating operations there, have tended to become bewildered about the benefits available to them and uncertain of their continuance. The CBI Regional Study, reporting on the effectiveness of Government inducements said: *The uncertainty of their duration and availability has led firms to discount them for the purposes of long-term planning.*

The point has been made several times in this book that Government action is the most unpredictable of all the factors with which industrialists have to contend. Regional policy is another case in point.

Cost of regional policy. Direct public expenditure on regional policies was £265 million in the financial year 1967–68,* and may well reach £300 million in 1968–69. The total cost of regional policies is undoubtedly much higher, because of the cost of various diseconomies imposed on industry and because of the cost of the

* Local Employment Acts 1960–66. 8th Annual Report of the Board of Trade, HMSO, August 1968.

side effects enumerated here. £500 million a year is probably a conservative estimate of the real current cost of regional policies. On similarly conservative estimates, it costs at least £1,000 from public funds to create a job in the development areas, plus a substantial contribution from the employer.

Such a massive diversion of resources to the less prosperous regions may conceivably be justifiable on social and political grounds. It would have some economic justification if it added a proportionate increment to national economic growth which would not otherwise occur, or if it produced self-perpetuating growth in the less prosperous regions and thus in due course ended the need for any special assistance to these regions. There is no evidence—so far, at least— that either of these economic aims are being achieved.

What should surely have been considered essential, before resources of the order of one per cent of GNP were committed, was the most extensive cost benefit analysis both of the measures proposed (including the cost of side effects) and of alternative measures. The CBI's Regional Survey claims that,

No attempt has been made to establish the negative cost of not taking other alternative measures; including those, for example, designed to ensure the continual growth of the prosperous regions.

Similarly, one would expect that the most careful consideration would have been given to ensuring that measures of regional policy dealt specifically with the real problems of the regions they are intended to help. In the view of a large and well-informed section of industrial opinion, this has not happened.

Failure to tackle the real problems. In the view of a massive majority of industrialists the fundamental problems of the less-prosperous regions are unavailability of suitably trained and experienced labour, particularly of key skilled craftsmen, and an inadequate infrastructure. The first of these problems gives rise to what the Scottish Council* has described as *the paradoxical situation of a relatively high unemployment rate and at the same time an inability on the part of many companies—both in new industries and in other industries, including labour-intensive industries—to recruit the workers they need for expansion.*

The two problems together constitute the major deterrents to industrialists in their location or expansion decisions. The CBI has reported: *The CBI's Regional Reports prove conclusively that the two principal obstacles to be overcome by a firm considering a move to a Development Area are the shortage of skilled or trainable labour*

* Scottish Council, Submission on the Regional Employment Premium, para. 16.

and the poor infrastructure. They show that the inducements offered by the Government are not a 'prime mover' influencing a firm's location decision.

If these conclusions are accepted, then the Government's policies and spending are misconceived. It is true that increasing resources are being devoted to training and retraining in development areas and that public works programmes in these areas have suffered fewer cuts and restrictions than elsewhere. The fact remains, however, that the resources devoted to training and improvement of infrastructure are minute compared with those (such as £100 million a year on the Regional Employment Premium, £46 million on BOT assistance and the estimated £75 million for the SET premium and investment grant differentials) devoted to the apparently ineffective inducements. Unless the CBI findings are wholly rejected, the conclusion must be drawn that in failing to pay due regard to the advice of industry and instead relying on the views of its theorists, the Government has wrongly diagnosed the problems of the less-prosperous regions and misapplied resources on a large scale.

SPECIFIC EFFECTS OF REGIONAL MEASURES

Apart from the side effects flowing from the Government's 'package' of regional measures, a number of others derive directly from specific measures. Two which seem especially important in national economic terms are considered here.

Regional Employment Premium. When the idea of the premium was mooted it was stated that:* *it would be essential that the premium payments should go primarily into reducing costs and prices rather than into extra wage increases.* Arguing that this would be achieved, the DEA and Treasury commented: *However, against the background of the relatively large unused labour resources in the Development Areas, there should be room for an appreciable rise in the demand for labour in those areas without causing excessive pressure on wage levels. Moreover, both sides of industry would have a responsibility to co-operate in ensuring that the object of the scheme—a reduction in labour costs—was not frustrated. It would be equally essential that this reduction in labour costs should be reflected in more competitive prices; experience suggests that in fact reduced costs are generally reflected in lower prices over a period of time.*

Evidence is accumulating to show that the critics and not the proponents of the premium were right. The CBI Regional Study states: *When CBI considered REP originally, members voiced the fear that REP would leak into wages. This is already happening in*

* Cmnd 3310.

Scotland and is having a particularly adverse effect on firms in Edinburgh which is outside the Development Area. *These fears have also been repeated in Wales and the North west, where it is suspected that with an upturn in activity they will be realised.* The dangers arising from the use of REP to give extra wage increases are twofold. First, they enable companies situated in the development areas to 'poach' employees from firms in adjoining areas, or alternatively compel such firms to indulge in a wages 'auction', resulting in either unjustified labour turnover or wage inflation. Second, any significant increase in wage levels in the development areas would act as a pacemaker for wage rises on a nationwide basis.

Industrial Development Certificates. These certificates provide the coercive element in the Government's regional 'package'. Since Labour came to power IDCs have been used with increasing stringency to divert new and expansion projects away from the South-east and Midlands and into the development areas, or the 'grey' areas, where they are freely issued. There are two important implications to this policy.

First, in so far as the use of IDCs is successful in diverting industrial projects, against companies' wishes, to development or 'grey' areas some definite diseconomies are imposed. These commonly include the costs of split management, duplicated services and higher transport costs.

Second, there can be no doubt that some companies when refused a development certificate in the area of their choice simply abandon the project they had in mind. The CBI staged a special survey on the effects of IDCs in the South-east and East Anglia and it found that twenty per cent of the schemes for which certificates were required were abandoned, deferred or modified because of the control, while only three and a half per cent of schemes were diverted to the development areas.

If this result can be regarded as in any way typical, it means that IDC's are causing at least a marginal loss of national economic growth without achieving significant results in diverting industry to the less prosperous regions. It is difficult to avoid the conclusion that the IDC system should be scrapped *in toto*.

CONCLUSIONS
State intervention to aid the less prosperous regions appears to have achieved a marginal effect in reducing the disparity between unemployment rates and industrial building in some development regions and those in Great Britain as a whole. This is the sole

discernible achievement to date, and it has been secured at great cost. The cost not only includes some £300 million a year from public funds, but the acceptance of a wide range of deleterious side effects. These include the subsidisation of inefficient firms, discouragement of rationalisation and labour mobility, industrial diseconomies arising from split locations, a possible increment of wage inflation and at least a marginal loss of national economic growth.

Since industry has already suffered from frequent shifts in regional policy measures, it would probably be unwise to contemplate immediate and dramatic changes in the entire present system. The Industrial Development Certificate system, however, appears on balance to be harmful, and could be scrapped without significant damage to regional policy.

There seems to be a strong case thereafter for switching emphasis away from the increasingly costly inducements the Government relies upon and towards the improvement of infrastructure and training facilities in the less prosperous regions. Such a switch, if sensibly planned in consultation with the regions and local authorities and not just arbitrarily announced from Great George Street would not only limit the present open-ended commitment on regional policy; it would also in due course eliminate many of the economic disadvantages of present policies and make a more realistic contribution to solving the undoubted problems of the less prosperous regions.

CHAPTER TWELVE

Capital investment, industrial structure and technology

Among the key elements in Labour's plans for revitalising Britain's economy were to be an increase in investment, an improvement in Britain's industrial structure, and the injection of modern technology into industry—dramatised by Mr Wilson as *the white hot technical revolution*. We have surveyed in Chapters 2, 3 and 6, the measures which the Government adopted in pursuit of these ends, and the hopes expressed by Ministers as these measures were introduced. We saw in Chapter 8 that the period 1964–68 was one of almost unrelieved economic failure. In this chapter we trace in detail the effects of Government policies and interventionist measures in those areas which Labour itself regarded as of key importance, and attempt to assess whether other measures, or less intervention, might have produced better results.

MANUFACTURING INVESTMENT
The table on pages 122 and 123 shows the course of fixed investment in Britain since 1960. The overall picture which it presents is far from satisfactory, either in the growth or distribution of investment. Total investment, including dwellings, which had risen by nineteen per cent in real terms between 1961 and 1964 rose by only thirteen per cent during the period 1964–68.

The most damaging feature to emerge from this table is the extremely disappointing progress of manufacturing investment. In 1967 and 1968 it was in real terms lower than the peak reached as long previously as 1961. This represents, of course, a sad failure of Labour's hopes. Of more importance, it also represents a highly serious setback to national economic progress, presaging capacity shortages with consequent damage to the balance of payments, and also indicating a slow rate of re-equipment with the most up to date plant and machinery. It should be added that in the autumn of 1968 a number of authorities, including the Board of Trade, were forecasting a fairly sharp upturn in fixed investment in 1969, amounting perhaps to a fifteen per cent improvement on the 1968 level. The generally cyclical nature of fixed investment, and the expected

FIXED INVESTME

| | | | Dwellings | | | | By type of asset | | |
		Total	Public	Private	Total	Total	Plant, mach-inery	Vehi-cles, ships, air-craft	B₁ in w₁
1957		867	79	76	155	712	331	130	2
1958		873	66	81	147	726	332	133	2
1959		942	68	100	168	774	346	145	2
1960		1,033	69	121	190	843	370	163	3
1961		1,131	72	132	204	927	421	152	3
1962		1,125	81	129	210	915	414	131	3
1963		1,145	86	128	214	931	432	137	3
1964		1,341	116	156	272	1,070	486	165	4
1965		1,395	123	154	277	1,118	518	162	4
1966		1,417	133	138	271	1,147	550	156	4
1967		1,507	153	145	298	1,209	571	167	4
1966	I	1,390	124	140	264	1,126	544	153	4
	II	1,408	130	143	273	1,135	547	156	4
	III	1,441	133	136	269	1,172	564	161	4
	IV	1,430	143	134	277	1,153	546	153	4
1967	I	1,460	147	135	282	1,178	560	161	4
	II	1,535	151	143	294	1,241	584	179	4
	III	1,515	154	151	305	1,210	574	161	4
	IV	1,518	159	151	310	1,208	564	169	4
1968	I	1,550	160	149	309	1,241	569	189	4
	II	1,516	159	158	317	1,199	530	177	4
	III	1,539	163	146	309	1,230	546	202	4

* Excluding legal fees, etc. (which are included in the other columns) of which the indu₁
† Excluding shipping which is included in other industries and services.

57-68

£ *million, 1958 prices, quarterly rates, seasonally adjusted*

Industries and services

By sector		By industry*				
ıblic	Private	Manu-facturing	Fuel, power	Public services	Transport, com-munica-tions†	Other indus-tries, services
298	414	244	118	74	85	181
405	421	230	123	82	80	200
331	443	218	137	93	84	230
341	502	254	131	98	93	254
370	557	299	138	117	91	270
378	537	275	149	137	80	262
395	536	241	174	144	80	279
449	621	273	199	170	88	326
467	651	301	208	177	95	323
502	645	308	234	187	95	308
568	641	301	249	216	108	321
475	651	310	224	176	93	310
495	640	305	232	185	92	307
523	649	311	248	192	97	310
514	639	307	233	196	98	306
545	633	300	248	196	106	314
565	676	313	253	218	106	336
578	632	295	251	224	108	318
585	623	295	245	227	111	316
593	648	288	230	239	119	349
575	624	289	209	241	125	320
561	669	303	200	238	125	348

tribution is not known.

Source: NIESR

effects of devaluation gave a good deal of credence to such predictions but they were thrown into considerable doubt by the 'mini-budget' of November 1968 which increased taxation of consumers' expenditure by some £250 million a year, imposed the imports deposit scheme, and savagely intensified the existing credit squeeze. Although there were some super-optimistic statements that the expected rise in fixed investment would still go ahead, the *Financial Times* Monthly Survey of Business Opinion in February 1969,* reported a substantial downward revision of capital spending plans. It accordingly seems probable that Labour's failure to stimulate manufacturing investment is going to continue for a further year.

This record is all the more melancholy because, whatever else may have been controversial in Labour's aims, the need for increased manufacturing investment in Britain has never been seriously disputed. Over most of the postwar period the proportion of Gross Domestic Product going into non-residential fixed investment in Britain has lagged far behind competing industrial nations.

The proportion was only two-thirds of that achieved by Germany and the Netherlands during the period 1955–64 and three-quarters of that achieved by France and Italy. Comparisons with Japan are even less favourable, showing Britain investing only half as much of its Gross Domestic Product as the Japanese.

These historical comparisons make the lag in manufacturing investment during the period 1964–68 all the more disappointing. Instead of catching up on our international competitors, we were falling behind. Manufacturing investment in Britain as a proportion of Gross Domestic Product even fell slightly from an average of 4·6 per cent during the period 1961–64 to 4·4 per cent during the period 1965–68. That this was not even keeping pace with current demand was evidenced by the appearance of substantial capacity shortages in important sectors such as synthetic fibres and PVC towards the end of 1968.

A DAUNTING CLIMATE FOR INVESTMENT

Anyone who knows how investment decisions are actually made in board rooms throughout the free world will have no difficulty in identifying the principal reasons for the lag in manufacturing investment under Labour. They do not hinge upon any one measure, but on the creation, through innumerable shifts of economic policy and a hodge-podge of restrictions and penalties on industrialists, of a climate in which only the safest or most urgently necessary kinds of fixed investment held any considerable attractions.

There are two key factors which determine investment decisions

* *Financial Times*, 3 February 1969.

in free enterprise business. The first of these is anticipated growth of demand. If industrialists think that there is a reasonable prospect that demand will grow steadily over the next few years they can plan to meet this growth with reasonable confidence that their investment will be requited with adequate profits. Some confidence in at least the continuation of the established rate of growth of demand is thus a precondition for investment: to secure any sharp upturn in industrial investment would require considerable confidence that the rate of growth of demand was itself going to increase. It should be observed here that for most businesses the key demand element is domestic demand. This is not to suggest that industrialists do not take export prospects into account in making their decisions: in a few cases they may be the paramount consideration. In general, however, ordinary business realism compels the industrialist to gear his investment decisions to domestic demand prospects because his export sales (even after devaluation) tend to be the most uncertain and least profitable element in the calculation. In most cases it is not just general domestic demand which is the key factor, but consumers' expenditure which provides the ultimate motivating force—even for sales of capital goods and other products apparently far removed from the consumer orbit.

The second crucial consideration which determines investment decisions is the fact that a decision *not* to invest is always 'safer' for a company than a decision to commit resources. Failure to seize an investment opportunity may in reality mean that the company foregoes profits it would otherwise have made, but this does not show up in the annual accounts: an investment which has gone wrong because the anticipated demand was not forthcoming or because selling prices were depressed shows a readily identifiable depression in the profits column.

One has only to survey the general course of economic events over the period 1964–68 to see how these two factors in combination were almost certain to keep industrial investment depressed. Virtually every one of Britain's numerous crises has been met by measures to restrain consumers' expenditure. Four of the five budgets introduced by Labour up to the end of 1968 included massive increases in indirect taxation, while the 'regulator' was applied in three 'mini-budgets'. A credit squeeze of mounting severity was in operation almost throughout the period, while the whole tenor of Government policy pronouncements consistently indicated determination to clamp down on domestic demand, and particularly on consumers' expenditure, whenever it showed signs of appreciable increase. Action of this kind may well have been unavoidable as the Government lurched from crisis to crisis, but it created a continuing situation in which managements had little incentive to commit themselves to new investment unless they were immediately short of capacity or believed they perceived some quite exceptional opportunity. The existence of very high interest rates throughout the period added considerably to the disincentive effect by putting a high cost on the service of capital, while a continuing and intensifying credit squeeze left many companies in doubt whether they would be able to obtain working capital when new investment projects came into operation.

In face of these powerful deterrents to investment there is perhaps little necessity to look for additional reasons for the disappointing record of the years 1964–68. There are, however, reasons for supposing that many of the Government's measures of intervention added either substantially or marginally to the disinclination to undertake fixed investment.

One factor which can reasonably be regarded as holding back new capital investment during the period was the rapidly growing vogue for mergers and takeovers. Later in this chapter we examine in some detail the effects of the Government's attempts to restructure British industry. It is a matter of factual record that merger and takeover activity accelerated enormously over the period 1964–68, though only a limited part of this acceleration was due to the direct and deliberate intervention of the Government or its agencies. Most of this 'merger mania', as journalists have described it, came about as a result of the general economic climate, and of the effects, probably unanticipated by the Government, of Mr Callaghan's so-called tax 'reforms' in the 1965 Budget.

Briefly, corporation tax made fixed-interest financing much more attractive to companies than equity financing, causing a shortage of equity shares which pushed up stock market prices and gave inflated values to company shares. Because of their high valuations, shares became an increasingly attractive medium for buying other companies and this effect was reinforced by the capital gains tax, which made companies' 'paper' more acceptable to shareholders than cash. It therefore became easy for companies to take each other over without having to find hard cash in the process. At the same time, the general economic climate made take-overs a more attractive form of expansion than 'green field' operations. A take-over is usually a much safer type of expansion than investment in new capacity. The take-over brings an existing share of the market and does not alter the demand/capacity situation; new capacity, on the other hand, requires an increase in overall demand for the product if it is to pay off.

It is quite certain that a good deal of effort which might have gone into new fixed investment during 1967 and 1968 instead went into mergers and take-overs because they had been made easier and because they involved less risk, in the economic circumstances of the time, than additions to capacity. The economy may eventually derive some benefits from the spate of mergers to the extent that they lead to rationalisation and elimination of obsolete or surplus capacity and to a more economic scale of operation. Eventually, no doubt, the merged companies will restart the process of fixed investment. In the meantime, however, the nation may suffer extensively from capacity shortages and lack of modernisation investment, and this will be an effect to which Government interventionist policies have directly contributed.

OTHER DEPRESSING FACTORS

There are several other forms of State intervention which must have further discouraged fixed capital investment. One of these is the Prices and Incomes Policy, particularly in its measures to control prices and dividends. Any form of price control is inevitably inimical to capital investment. If there is any prospect that the products from a new plant will have to be sold at arbitrarily low prices, the payoff from the investment is open to a high degree of uncertainty and is likely to be unattractive. Equally, among other justifications for a company to undertake physical expansion is the hope of being able to pay higher dividends to its shareholders. Permanent and artificial limitation of dividends is bound to diminish the incentive to expand, and the greater the risks attaching to expansion the greater will be the disincentive effect of dividend limitation.

It seems certain that the Government's regional policies have also had an effect in limiting fixed capital investment. The tough application of the IDC policy to prevent expansion in the South-east and the Midlands has not just transferred a corresponding amount of fixed investment elsewhere. As the CBI enquiries have shown, a good deal of projected investment which has run into IDC troubles has simply been deferred or abandoned.* This effect may have been partially offset by some projects going ahead in the development areas because the various subsidies available there have made them viable when they would not otherwise have been. Such projects, of course, add to the total of fixed investment undertaken, though, as was suggested in the previous chapter, projects which only survive with the aid of big State subsidies do not necessarily constitute the most economic means of employing the nation's resources.

Another depressant to fixed investment has been the Government's discrimination against service industries, through the medium of

* Regional development and distribution of industry policy, Confederation of British Industry, September 1968.

investment grants, regional policies, and SET. The result of this discrimination must have been to reduce investment in service industries and service facilities to a figure well below what it would otherwise have been. Presumably such an outcome is supposed to be beneficial to the nation according to the theories of some of the Government's advisers, but it has resulted in a considerable depression of fixed capital spending in Britain. Few industrialists can perceive the logic of deterring investment which would make the service industries more efficient.

It would be surprising if, in addition to the specific effects of intervention already considered, the cumulative psychological effects of a climate of increasing restriction and intervention did not constitute a considerable deterrent to the risky process of fixed investment. The industrialist contemplating physical expansion already has to face major degrees of uncertainty arising from the normal processes of the competitive market economy. The effect of growing intervention is to add massive elements of further uncertainty—the more intervention is being resorted to, the more likely it becomes that the ground rules will have been arbitrarily changed between the time when the decision to invest is made and the time, which may be several years, when the product comes on the market. In an economic climate which already contains a high degree of uncertainty, industrialists would hardly be rational if they welcomed still further elements of uncertainty arising from the possibilities of State intervention. The more uncertain the situation, the higher the probability that the industrialist will stay uncommitted.

INDUSTRIAL STRUCTURE

Both before the 1964 Election and in office, Labour Party spokesmen have talked frequently and at considerable length about 'basic industrial and technological reconstruction'. By the time of its 'mid-term manifesto' in September 1968,* the Party was claiming that a revival of the British economy was on the way and attributed it to: *the result of firm action taken earlier to achieve industrial modernisation and reconstruction—to bring about a transformation of the debilitated economic structure we inherited into one capable of responding to, and taking advantage of the technological revolution through which the world is living.*

Are such claims justifiable? Has British industry really been modernised and reconstructed during the period 1964-68? In so far as modernisation and reconstruction has taken place, to what extent is this simply the result of natural economic forces, and to what extent is it due to encouragement given and measures specifically

* *Britain: Progress and Change*, Labour Party, 1968.

undertaken by the Government? It is a matter of factual record that merger and takeover activity has massively increased since 1964. Such activity notified to the Board of Trade during 1964 was around £300 million; by 1968 merger and takeover activity was proceeding at a rate of about £1,000 million of capital assets per year. It seems probable that between the General Election in October 1964 and the end of 1968, mergers and takeovers involving capital assets of over £2,500 million took place.

Of this vast tide of activity only a relatively small proportion occurred at the direct behest of the Government or its agent, the Industrial Reorganisation Corporation. The most spectacular of such direct interventions were the merger of the Leyland Motor Corporation and British Motor Holdings, in which the IRC played a substantial part and committed £25 million, and the merger between International Computers and Tabulators and the data processing interests of English Electric to form International Computers Limited, which was effected under the Industrial Expansion Act, with the Ministry of Technology committing £17 million. Another major series of mergers taking place as the result of Government initiative occurred in the shipbuilding industry under the aegis of the Ministry of Technology. The IRC played a fairly significant part in a number of other small mergers, including English Electric/Elliott-Automation, Dunford & Elliott Hatfields, the Nuclear Enterprises series of acquisitions, British Oxygen Company/Edwards High Vacuum, the Davy Ashmore Acquisitions, and the Whessoe Acquisition.* Other mergers or takeovers in which the IRC had some interest were GEC/AEI, Coats Patons/West Riding Worsted and W. H. Allen/Belliss & Morecom, though it is probably fair to assume that all these would have gone ahead on normal commercial principles without the IRC's blessing, and irrespective of whether the corporation had existed or not. The later merger between GEC/AEI and English Electric falls into the same category.

Adding in such notorious IRC activities as its role in promoting the Kent–Cambridge Instruments merger and frustrating the Rank Organisation's bid, does not amount to 'transformation' of Britain's industrial structure in any meaningful sense of the term. Nor does a spate of mergers largely prompted by tax-induced special Stock Market factors and undertaken as a deliberate substitute for new capital investment constitute a particular triumph for the economy. A broadly similar merger boom in the USA during recent years has certainly produced no ecstatic talk about 'industrial restructuring'. On the contrary, the authorities have taken steps to check it.

* Industrial Reorganisation Corporation, First Report and Accounts (December 1966–March 1968), HMSO.

I

Several percipient observers have pointed out the damage which may result from an uncontrolled rush of mergers. Anthony Harris, the Economics Editor of the *Guardian* has shown, for example, how bid situations lead to short-sighted management with restrictions on research and capital spending.* It was apparent that in the early months of 1969 the President of the Board of Trade, Mr Anthony Crosland, had taken fright at the continued merger boom when he halted a batch of proposed unions, including Unilever–Allied Breweries, Rank–de la Rue, and Courtaulds–English Calico, pending further investigations.

Ever since the Industrial Revolution, British industry has been progressively altering its structure by merger and takeover in response to normal market forces. Some of the alterations have been damaging and some irrelevant, but the overall effects have been beneficial. Much the same judgment will doubtless eventually be passed on the big burst of merger activity which characterised Labour's term of office. There is no obvious reason to suppose that the relatively small proportion of mergers promoted by the Government or the IRC will turn out to be more beneficial to the economy than those brought about by genuine market forces.

THE MISSING TECHNOLOGICAL REVOLUTION

One persistent theme expounded by Britain's post-war leaders is that technology can be its major resource—the twentieth-century equivalent of nineteenth-century coal. Prime Minister Harold Wilson's election promise of a 'white-hot technical revolution' was the strongest statement of the need for a bold use of technology made by all the post-war prime ministers. To date, the rhetoric has not been matched by deeds, for there have been no major steps towards the development of technology and its application to British industry.

This uncomprising statement comes from the authoritative and objective Brookings Report on the British economy published in September 1968.† It probably represents fairly enough the consensus of informed opinion on the progress made under Labour in the technological field.

Nobody can be happy that a perfectly laudable intention to bring about a dramatic improvement in Britain's technological competence has so far produced fairly minimal fruits. What has been attempted requires careful analysis to try to determine whether it has been adequate in quantity, correct in conception and execution, or whether some other forms of action might have produced better

* 'How takeovers hurt the economy', *Guardian*, 15 January 1969.
† *Britain's Economic Prospects*, Brookings Institution (George Allen & Unwin), 1968.

results. It is equally worth considering whether a 'technical revolution' in the sense that Mr Wilson presumably intended—that is, a dramatically rapid upsurge in Britain's exploitation of the most advanced technology—was ever feasible within the economic and political constraints of the second half of the 1960s.

The idea that a 'technical revolution' is possible must stem from the thesis that there is a substantial amount of technological slack to be taken up in British industry. In hypothetical terms this is a credible enough proposition. Nobody could seriously argue that all the available technological opportunities are being exploited, either in the form of producing new technology-based goods, or in the universal adoption of the most advanced available manufacturing methods. In practice, of course, no nation ever approaches the point of 100 per cent exploitation of all the available technological opportunities. To do so would mean that as every new advance was made the existing plant and machinery in a particular field would be scrapped and new equipment installed. Similarly all manufacturers would have to abandon existing products as soon as the possibility of making improved products became available. What happens in even the most advanced nations is a gradual switch to new and improved processes, and a gradual adoption of innovation products. The speed at which new technology can be adopted inevitably depends upon the availability of capital for investment. New technology is normally highly research-intensive and highly capital-intensive. It often has an extremely long pay-off period and carries high risk arising from the possibility of rapid technological obsolescence of both product and process.

Judgment on the scope for a 'technical revolution' in Britain must therefore rest on two factors. The first of these is the extent to which we are developing and exploiting the most up to date technology relative to our international competitors. On this basis there can be little doubt that we are lagging behind the United States, but there is certainly no conclusive evidence that we generally lag behind our European competitors. This is a difficult factor to measure, but one indicator is the proportion of research-intensive products in total industrial output compared with that of other nations. The table on page 132 shows comparative figures for the 1950s which do not suggest that we were then out of line with our international competitors in the exploitation of research-intensive products. It would be interesting to see more up to date figures, but there is no reason to suppose that the share of 'A' group products in our industrial output has fallen, though the proportion of these products may have increased in the output of some competing nations.

Another indirect measure of the exploitation of technology derives from productivity comparisons. Here, of course, Britain compares very badly with the United States, and generally comes out marginally worse than our European competitors. Productivity comparisons, however, are only the roughest indication of technological competence. They measure the intensity and efficiency of use of plant and processes and not just its technical efficiency. There is undoubtedly scope on a very large scale for Britain to increase productivity by the use of more up to date machinery and processes, but we also need to use the equipment we already possess much more efficiently.

If this is a correct assessment of the situation, it implies that there may be considerably less scope for achieving a dramatic upsurge in national wealth through the more vigorous and intelligent application of technology than is popularly supposed. The scope is in any case inevitably limited by the investment resources available. Even if the highly optimistic growth and investment assumptions of the 1965 National Plan had been achieved, the investment resources

PERCENTAGE OF GNP ORIGINATING IN MANUFACTURING, 1964, AND DISTRIBUTION OF INDUSTRIAL OUTPUT BY RESEARCH-INTENSITY INDUSTRY GROUP, EIGHT COUNTRIES, 1949–59 AVERAGE

Country†	Percentage of GNP originating in manufacturing, 1964	Percentage distribution by research-intensity industry group*		
		Group A	Group B	Group C
United Kingdom ..	36	49·6	19·9	30·5
United States ..	30	48·0	21·4	30·6
Germany	41	44·8	19·7	35·5
France‖	36	44·0	10·1	45·9
Netherlands ..	n.a.	41·5	14·4	44·1
Italy	32	40·7	14·4	44·9
Norway	26	34·1	25·1	40·8
Belgium¶	30	33·0	22·9	44·1

* OECD classification, in which industries are divided into Groups A, B and C by descending order of research intensity.
† Ranked in order of percentage of industrial output in Group A.
‖ Fishing and production of building materials included in manufacturing. Paper, printing, and publishing are in Group C instead of Group B, because of data limitations.
¶ Gas included in manufacturing.
n.a. Not available.

Sources: Percentage of GNP originating in manufacturing for each country from US Bureau of the Census, *Statistical Abstract of the United States: 1966*, p. 905. Industry distribution computed from data on average shares in manufacturing output from 1949 to 1959 as contained in United Nations, Economic Commission for Europe, *Economic Survey of Europe in 1961*, Pt. 2, *Some Factors in Economic Growth in Europe during the 1950s* (Geneva, 1964), p. 12.

available would not have been sufficient to enable Britain to exercise world leadership in technology on more than a very narrow front.

The implication is that the idea of a 'technical revolution' was grossly oversold by Mr Wilson in the run up to the 1964 General Election. Any sensible evaluation of the Government's intervention to secure more effective and profitable application of advanced technology needs to discount the political rhetoric and to assess what has been done against what was, on a common sense view, genuinely possible. What has been attempted can be conveniently classified under three headings. The first of these embraces the attempts to reorganise and redirect under a single Minister the whole corpus of Government-run research. A second group comprises what show business would call the 'spectaculars': this includes major technological projects, such as Concorde and atomic energy, and big structural reorganisations of industries with a technological content, such as computers, shipbuilding, and motor vehicles. A third group of activities comprises the generally unspectacular business of trying to persuade British industry to adopt more advanced processes.

REORGANISATION OF GOVERNMENT RESEARCH

We have already seen (Chapter 2) that one of the results of the establishment of the Ministry of Technology was a massive re-shuffling of ministerial responsibilities for Government controlled research and development establishments. The resources involved were very substantial, including around 9,000 qualified engineers and scientists—approximately one-sixth of the total graduate population employed on research and development work in Britain. The Ministry has stated that this is the largest body of research and development staff employed under a single direction in Europe.

The stated aims of this reorganisation were wholly laudable. It was intended to promote both more purposeful and economic direction of activities and to ensure that the results achieved by this research and development activity, and the expertise available in Government establishments, were made more freely and effectively available to British industry.

Progress with the first of these aims is difficult to measure. There have undoubtedly been substantial changes in the programmes and activities of many of the units brought under the Ministry of Technology's control, and a wide variety of new projects and services of potential value to industry have been added. Some of these changes and additions would no doubt have come about in the normal course of events, but many of them have resulted from the existence of over-all direction aimed at increasing the industrial usefulness of R & D work. Among the more imaginative measures in this field has been the setting up of the Ministry's Programmes Analysis Unit. The need for such a unit was described by the Ministry in the following terms:* *Because the costs of research and development are increasing rapidly, there is a growing awareness worldwide of the need to assess the effectiveness of resource use on as comprehensive and rigorous a basis as possible. The choice of areas of activity for research and development require economic studies of the components of the industrial and social system, and a prediction of the probable interactions of technological change with social and economic needs. The costs and benefits likely to arise from particular activities must be systematically analysed, bearing in mind that the principal national objectives of any investment are to increase national wealth, and to improve the balance of payments position of the United Kingdom.*

The kind of questions the Unit is required to answer were listed by the Ministry as follows:*

(a) Are there areas of technology where more R & D would lead to benefits, and can these be quantified?

(b) What R & D resources can justifiably be applied to particular fields of economic or social importance?

(c) What contribution would R & D make to the achievement of specific industrial objectives?

(d) What is the optimum portfolio of R & D within a given field?

(e) What are the costs and benefits of doing a particular proposed research and development programme? To what extent should the programme be supported with Government funds?

Objective answers to such questions, sensibly translated into practice, might help to prevent problems of the kind the Ministry of Technology currently faces in some of its 'spectaculars'. To be fair, most of these activities, such as the QE2 and Concorde were inherited from the preceding administration. The obvious problems —uncontrollably soaring costs, lengthening time scales, and a highly dubious ultimate commercial pay-off—tend to be characteristic of government-sponsored technological prestige projects in many countries.

A more serious underlying problem which arises when governments allow themselves to be drawn into massive projects which would not attract ordinary commercial support is the pre-emption of resources which could be better used elsewhere. One immediate example is the Government's withdrawal from ELDO and its generally minimal commitment to the exploitation of satellite communications, which would presumably not have occurred if the

* *New Technology*, No. 16, April 1968.

enormously expensive undertakings on Concorde and other projects had not existed. In more general terms, massive support by successive governments for Britain's aircraft and defence industries has led to a disproportionate concentration of our scientific resources.

One of the fundamental problems in large-scale Government intervention in technological matters, especially those involving substantial cash or human resources, is decision-making on questions of balance and choice of projects. Should the Ministry spread its resources thinly (and therefore probably ineffectively) over the whole field of technological endeavour? Should it select a few fields of activity and provide them with the kind of resources necessary for a decisive breakthrough, risking that other fields, which may prove more rewarding in the long run, may be neglected in the process? Having selected fields for support, should help be given to all candidates in these fields? If not, how does the Ministry select the potential winners?

One does not have to be a dogmatic opponent of State involvement in industry to suspect that ministers and their advisers are worse equipped to make such decisions than industry, which after all earns its profits by the practice of technology. Such a view has been expressed by Mr John Duckworth, managing director of the Government's own National Research Development Corporation. In a recent speech* he argued that: *the heavy concentration of Government expenditure in some areas without the application of normal commercial 'criteria' had had a disadvantageous effect on the economy.*

He also claimed that the Government was trying to diversify its efforts to encourage innovation and to use Government establishments to greater advantage, but said it had not found a way of using its resources effectively.

Mr Duckworth said that private industry was better equipped than the Government to select the areas of technology where future applied research and development would be most rewarding, as industry knew the markets.

He said: 'Government must first create the environment in which industry will do as much as possible itself—and then find effective means of supporting specific long-term and large projects without itself too closely calling the tune.'

There was no real evidence that publicly controlled bodies, including the nationalised industries, had shown any greater ability to innovate than private industry.

Indeed, the difficulties inherent in relationships between monopoly purchasers and their suppliers, and the inertia of large organisations

* Reported in *The Times* and *Financial Times*, 14 April 1969.

*exposed to conflicting policies rather than normal commercial pressures,
have on the whole had the opposite effect.*

There is nothing unusual about such views among people inti-
mately acquainted with the technological scene. The implication is
clear. A massive and detailed Government involvement in technology
is unlikely to bring benefit to the nation. Government support for
technology is best calculated to bring benefits if it is applied through
projects chosen and implemented by industry itself.

One might, indeed, go further and ask if the 'technical revolution'
might not best be speeded by leaving much more money to bear
fruit within industry itself, instead of collecting ever-increasing
amounts in the spiral of taxation so that they can be doled out on
projects chosen, on something other than commercial grounds, by
the Ministry.

Certainly most solutions favoured by people who understand the
application of technology would involve a reduction in the role of
the Ministry of Technology, leaving it with sponsorship and persuasive functions, the operation of small-scale interventionist
services which industry felt to be genuinely useful, and the direction
of such Government-financed research as might on evaluation be
considered worthy of survival.

MORE FUNDAMENTAL PROBLEMS

If this evaluation is correct, it seems probable that the Government's
intervention through the Ministry of Technology has brought a
number of minor benefits. Reorganisation and redirection of the
large Government-controlled R & D effort has already brought
about some improved co-operation with industry, and the long
term efforts of the Programmes Analysis Unit may well be very
beneficial in harnessing Government-financed scientific work to
projects with the maximum potential pay off.

The productivity advisory services and other measures to popularise the use of more advanced technology have met with varying
success, but it is to be expected that overall they have made some
contribution to the technological competence of industry. They
have also given some practical help and encouragement to some
producers of advanced equipment.

The more spectacular ventures in big prestige projects, in international collaboration, and particularly in industrial restructuring,
are much more uncertain in their effects. Some of them, as we have
seen, may prove wasteful and some may prove misconceived and
potentially damaging.

Even if one takes the most optimistic view of the outcome of all
the work done by the Ministry of Technology, it is difficult to avoid

the conclusion, which many industrialists put forward, that the sum total of all the Ministry's efforts only adds up to the most marginal help at the fringes of Britain's real technological problems. What it has signally failed to do is to touch the more fundamental problems which really hold back Britain's progress as a major technological power. Not only has no progress been made in solving these problems by the Ministry of Technology; there is massive evidence that the Government's intervention in other fields, particularly through economic management and taxation, has enormously hampered technological progress in Britain.

On this view the absolutely fundamental factor limiting the exploitation of technology is profitability. Inadequate industrial profitability limits the exploitation of technology in two ways. First, it means that those capable of advanced innovation have inadequate resources available for activities generally characterised by high risk, high capital intensivity, and a long pay-off period. At the same time low profitability means a poor home market for innovation equipment and processes: companies can only be expected to replace obsolescent equipment and adopt new processes if their cash flows are providing the necessary funds.

The after-tax profitability of British companies is approximately one-third lower than that of American companies, according to comparisons between *Fortune* and *Management Today's* profitability tables. This difference provides by far the most credible explanation why American industry is far more willing and able to pioneer new products, to adopt new manufacturing methods, and to re-equip with the most up to date plant and machinery than British industry.

The sum total of Government economic policy, particularly of tax policy over Labour's term of office, has been to perpetuate and intensify the profit-earning difficulties of British industry. This arises in numerous ways, particularly from the over-all size of the tax burden, from changes in its incidence, from the various forced loan effects, and from the general air of uncertainty which so many shifts and changes have engendered. Apart from holding down profitability, the Government policy of restricting dividends, increasing taxation on capital gains and generally discouraging savings, has inevitably restricted the flow of capital to the expensive and risky function of technological innovation.

This has especially been the case with small companies and individual entrepreneurs who might otherwise have brought about important additions to the nation's technological base. Informed observers often bemoan the fact that Britain has few developments comparable with those of the growth of small technologically advanced companies on America's Route 128. Given the close company regulations, dividend restriction, and the deliberate destruction of stock options, it is not surprising that beneficial development of this kind has hardly taken place in Britain. To quote a distinguished tax consultant:* *Invention is a creative process, unlikely to be either deterred or encouraged by fiscal considerations. The next stage, commercial development, involves considerable investment, a less exciting period of attention to detail and a long wait for uncertain rewards. This is an entrepreneurial function, undertaken by the inventor himself, a private angel or a public company with a cold financial eye on the hope of profit and the risk of loss. The British tax system biases the odds against this. The mobile owner of a valuable talent can, once he reaches the top UK rate of surtax, obtain up to eleven times the net reward for his talent by emigrating. Even if there were no specially unfavourable features in the tax treatment of inventors, the man with a new idea would find it much easier to get development backing in other countries—and far more profitable to take himself abroad as well.* He went on to add: *The tax treatment of inventors urgently needs amending. We have the creative talent: let us encourage it to develop and flourish here instead of stifling it with restrictions and penalties or banishing it in search of more hospitable jurisdictions.*

Closely allied to this particular problem is the problem of the 'brain drain'. In the days when the Labour Party was talking so persuasively about the 'technical revolution' it also promised action to stop or ameliorate the net loss of qualified manpower through migration. In fact, it has been estimated that the gross outflow of engineers and scientists rose from 3,200 in 1961 to 6,200 in 1966. In addition 2,000 managers emigrated during 1966; emigration of managers has almost as direct an impact on the nation's technological capability, since managerial abilities are at least as important in technological development as the input of scientific skills.

The discouragement of the development of small technology-based companies, and failure to provide a more attractive environment for our technological manpower resources constitute factors which are inevitably likely to slow the development of advanced products and processes in Britain. A third factor, which has already been examined in this chapter, is the failure of Government measures to stimulate investment and the total effects of Government policy in discouraging risk-taking.

The low level of capital investment over the period 1964-68 is likely to have damaged technological advance more than any other business activity. If businessmen are being cautious about investment, the fields they are most likely to avoid are those where risk is high

* John Chown, *Financial Times* Annual Review of British Industry, 8 July 1968.

and payoff is likely to be long delayed. These, almost by definition, are the characteristics of advanced technology projects.

A gloomy climate for investment has effects well beyond the reduction of the commitment of resources to new, advanced plant, processes and products. As a distinguished businessman, Robert Appleby,* has shown, it also reduces 'revenue investment'. This is the investment, in process development, improved planning and work flow techniques, and improved management technology generally, which is at least as essential to international competitiveness in industry, as investment in physical resources. Figures for the course of revenue investment in British industry are hard to come by, but there is reason to suppose that company managements hold down revenue investment during times of uncertainty in much the same way as they restrict fixed capital investment. It is probable that inadequate capital investment during the period 1964–68 has been matched by inadequate revenue investment, and that this has been another factor holding back the application and development of advanced technology in Britain.

What we have so far considered in no sense exhausts the large range of fundamental problems restricting technological advance. There are in addition important problems of balance and manpower shortage. So far as balance is concerned, the most publicised problems in Britain have been the high proportion of scientific resources devoted to the aircraft industry and to military research and development. Another problem of balance is the high proportion, relative to other nations, and particularly to our European competitors, of basic and fundamental research in the national science and technology effort. Most observers (see, for example, the Brookings Institution Report) suggest that a major correction of these imbalances could add substantially to the performance of British industry generally. This is a complex problem, if only because some of the manpower resources involved are resistant to forced change of industry. The outcome of the major and disruptive changes imposed by the Government on the aircraft industry in 1965 was not a redistribution of personnel to other British industries, but a rapid acceleration of the 'brain drain' to American aerospace companies. Similarly any dramatic reduction in basic research in Britain would be likely to result in increased emigration of those attracted by the fascinations of this activity. It was not to be expected that the Ministry of Technology could find solutions to these difficult problems of balance overnight, but it is, perhaps, a legitimate criticism that so little progress has been made over four years. One of the claims usually made for State intervention is that it can

* Robert Appleby, British Institute of Management National Conference, 1966.

bring about desirable change more quickly and effectively than market forces. The Ministry's failure to make any apparent contribution to the problems of restoring balance in our scientific effort hardly supports this thesis.

The major problem in the distribution of Britain's scientific manpower is a critical shortage of engineers relative to scientists. Most of our industrial competitors employ around three engineers for every natural scientist: in Britain the proportion is approximately five to four. This has serious implications in terms of the commercial exploitation of scientific advance. Obviously one way of improving this situation, though long term in effect, is to increase the supply of engineers from the educational system. This is being done, though not, the Brookings Report suggests, on a sufficiently large scale. Another approach is to improve the status of the professional engineer and the attractions of a career in engineering. The Ministry of Technology has made some modest moves on the status problem, but Britain's low standing in net executive and professional remuneration is ensuring a continuation of the 'brain drain' of our scarce engineering resources.

SOME CONCLUSIONS

Nobody would dispute the desirability of more intensive exploitation of technology in Britain. Unfortunately there is little reason to conclude that, despite its grandiose promises, the Labour Government has made any substantial improvement. This is not primarily due to any major inadequacies in the Ministry of Technology (though some of its activities may be dubiously beneficial). The failure to achieve any striking improvement in the exploitation of technology during the period 1964-68 is largely due to the general network of policies and measures which have depressed business activity and slowed economic growth.

The measures most likely to encourage rapid technological development are really those which would encourage business activity generally. A Government programme which gave top priority to enabling industry to earn higher profits and to retain more of them after the tax 'take' would undoubtedly give more stimulus to technological development and the modernisation of British industry than all the activities of the Ministry of Technology.

CHAPTER THIRTEEN

Effects of an interventionist climate

The most persistent and vociferous criticisms of state intervention in industry do not relate to specific measures or policies, but to the alleged general and psychological effects of a mounting tide of Government interference and control. Burgeoning bureaucracy, proliferating civil servants, excessive form-filling, unfair and arbitrary discrimination between industries and companies, and absurdly conflicting official policies are among the familiar indictments. Coupled with rising taxation, sometimes imposed for interventionist reasons, they are alleged to diminish or destroy incentives to effort and enterprise.

It almost goes without saying that there are frequently elements of political and ideological bias or of special pleading in such criticisms. This does not make them unimportant. Their sheer frequency and vehemence suggests, *prima facie*, that they must have some factual foundation. At the very least they imply that there may be remediable defects in certain types of intervention.

There is a much wider significance, however, in repeated complaints about 'stultifying bureaucracy' and 'lack of incentive'. If businessmen believe, rightly or wrongly, that such conditions exist, the belief is likely to shape their actions and attitudes. It is particularly likely to affect willingness to take risks or to put in extra effort. Given Britain's crucial dependence on the zeal and judgment of a relatively small number of industrial leaders, any significant diminution of enterprise or motivation has potentially serious national implications.

This chapter, then attempts to assess both the 'micro' and 'macro' effects of a climate of growing state intervention. The assessment is inevitably tentative. It deals with areas in which statistics are few and opinions many. It attempts to trace the often tenuous links between belief and action. It does, however, raise one crucial question which every interventionist-minded politician or civil servant ought to consider: the extent to which bureaucratic escalation and psychological reaction may make well-meaning intervention either worthless or actually harmful to the national interest.

BURGEONING BUREAUCRACY?

There is no accepted measure of increasing (or decreasing) bureaucracy. It is not difficult, however, to suggest some commonsense criteria.

Most people feel themselves involved in increasing bureaucracy if, in pursuing their ordinary legitimate business, they are required increasingly to notify or seek approval from Government departments or agencies. On this account, industry's exposure to bureaucracy has undoubtedly increased sharply. Since 1964, new or extended requirements for notification and/or approval have been applied to:

Price increases
Wage and salary increases
Dividend increases ⎬ Prices and Incomes Acts, 1966–68
Capital distributions

Industrial building ⎱ Through reduction of exemption
Office building ⎰ limits on IDCs. Control of Office & Industrial Development Act 1965

Takeovers and mergers   Powers to refer to Monopolies Commission

Goods transport   Transport Act, 1968 (quantity licensing provisions not yet in force)

The above list is not exhaustive. Many individual industries, such as building and pharmaceuticals, have in addition, been subjected to new controls during the period.

Another criterion of increasing bureaucracy is multiplication of the Government departments or agencies authorised to intervene in the business of the citizen. Here, too, there has been a sharp increase during the period under review.

Two new ministries, Mintech and the DEA have been created with specific responsibilities for intervening in industrial matters. The old Ministry of Labour has been transformed into the Department of Employment and Productivity and given substantial powers for intervention under the Prices and Incomes Policy. The Treasury has assumed powers to intervene on dividend increases and capital distributions, while four ministries (the Board of Trade, Agriculture, Transport and Power) have authority to intervene on price questions.

In addition, a substantial range of Government-supported agencies have been set up with powers to demand or urge action, exact levies or request information from industry. They include the National Board for Prices and Incomes, the Industrial Reorganisation Corporation, the Land Commission, the twenty-five industry training boards (set up under the Industrial Training Act passed by the previous Conservative administration) and the 'little Neddies'.

One of the hallmarks of bureaucracy, in the view of many observers, is the vesting of increasing discretionary powers in politicians, civil servants and Government agencies. The effect of such an increase is to enlarge uncertainty. When the forms and details of intervention are strictly prescribed by law, those likely to be affected know, with reasonable certainty, what to expect. If considerable freedom of choice is left to the Government's agent, then it becomes a matter of guesswork whether there will be intervention and what form it will take.

There has been a substantial increase in discretionary powers during the period 1964–68. Increased restrictions on the issue of Industrial Development Certificates and office building have widened the discretionary powers of the Board of Trade. Much of the assistance given to industry by 'sponsoring ministries' is on a discretionary basis. The National Board for Prices and Incomes has wide discretionary limits (subject only to whatever Government-imposed 'criteria' happen to be in force) in delivering its judgments. The Industrial Reorganisation Corporation, as we have seen, has virtually unlimited powers to intervene, at its discretion anywhere in industry: it does not, of course, have powers of compulsion, but it has the next-best thing—very big funds which it can deploy on terms which industry, at least, would not recognise as strictly commercial.

Somewhat akin to administrative discretion are powers for ministers to impose their wishes by statutory instrument. Such powers have been a feature of much of the Labour Government's legislation affecting industry, notably the Prices and Incomes Acts (1966–68), the Industrial Expansion Act, and the Control of Office and Industrial Development Act 1965.

NEW OFFENCES AND PENALTIES

Laws have to be enforced, so it is an inevitable feature of state intervention in industry that new classes of offence are created. The Prices and Incomes Acts have created a variety of new offences for which both employers and trade unionists can be fined, including the offence of failing to give information to the National Board for Prices and Incomes when summoned to do so. Similarly, the Control of Office and Industrial Development Act 1965, created two new offences: proceeding with operations after an enforcement notice has been served, and failing to give information to the Board of Trade when required.

Of much more widespread and serious impact has been the practice of the Labour Government of loading heavy fiscal penalties on business for acts which were formerly regarded as innocuous, if not praiseworthy. The most notorious example, as we have seen, was Mr Callaghan's 1965 Finance Act which, *inter alia*, penalised companies for:

> Distributing dividends
> Making profits overseas
> Being 'close' (i.e. under the control of five or fewer participators, or of participators who are directors)

Another example is Selective Employment Tax, which penalises companies for employing people in non-manufacturing occupations or being in particular ('service') lines of business.

Also to be mentioned in this context are the forced loans exacted from industry and business. Historically, forced loans were a bone of contention between 'people' and Crown, and nowadays they are more associated with dictatorships and 'banana republics' than with advanced democratic nations. However, they have returned to Britain in the form of Selective Employment Tax, which forces manufacturing industry to provide an interest-free revolving loan of around £400 million to the Government, and the Import Deposits Scheme (new in 1968) which exacts an interest-free six-month loan (estimated to total £600 million at peak) from those importing goods into Britain.

DISCRIMINATION BETWEEN COMPANIES AND INDUSTRIES

It is difficult for a government to intervene in industry on any substantial scale without discriminating between particular companies and industries, particularly if the forms of intervention allow considerable administrative discretion. Some forms of discrimination were virtually traditional in Britain long before Labour returned to power: the discrimination implicit, for example, in different rates of purchase tax or excise duties, and in the effects on the motor and durable goods industries of using hire-purchase controls as an economic regulator. It has also been quite customary for British Governments to select certain industries for special help when they run into employment-jeopardising troubles: the various measures taken to rescue the cotton industry are one example, while the willingness of successive governments to stand continuous losses from some of the nationalised industries, rather than let them contract to economic size constitutes another.

What Mr Wilson's administration has done is to maintain almost

all the traditional forms of discrimination, while introducing a rapid
succession of schemes and measures deliberately or coincidentally
involving further discrimination.

We have already looked at some of these deliberate measures of
discrimination. The discrimination, for example, between manufacturing and service industries involved in SET, investment grants, and
the regional employment premium (and quite clearly based on the
disputed theories of Dr Nicholas Kaldor), also the various types of
discrimination involved between companies operating in the development areas and those outside (particularly those only just outside)
their borders. Another substantial body who feel themselves to be
the victims of deliberate discrimination are small businesses. The
most immediate irritant here is probably the close company legislation but a variety of other measures, ranging from the Industrial
Training Act to the promotion of structural change appear to bear
more harshly on the small company than on its bigger brethren.
Companies whose main business was overseas, and the big groups
with substantial foreign investments, are in no doubt they are
suffering deliberate discrimination through changes in the tax
treatment of overseas income introduced in the 1965 Finance Act.
Deliberate discrimination (in the form of state subsidised competition)
is also expected by companies likely to suffer from schemes to
extend the nationalised industries' manufacturing and trading
activities.

Coincidental discrimination arises almost inevitably from Government attempts to define the terms on which it will levy taxes or
give subventions or impose restrictions. The selection of product
groups for action under the Prices and Incomes Policy, for example,
or for treatment under the 1965 Imports Surcharge and the 1968
Imports Deposit Scheme inevitably involves varying degrees of
hardship between different industries and different companies. The
operation of the IDC scheme can impose much harsher penalties on
the small company (which may not be able to afford split locations)
than on the big company already organised to operate on a number
of sites.

The loudest complaints of discrimination occur when Government
departments or agencies load the scales for or against individual
companies. One controversial example was the Government's
rescue of the Fairfield shipbuilding yard from bankruptcy in 1965.
The worst offenders in inter-company discrimination, however, are
the Industrial Reorganisation Corporation, with its virtually un-
restricted terms of reference. Its intervention on behalf of George
Kent and against the Rank Organisation in the 1968 takeover battle
for Cambridge Instruments was not only condemned as such by

many industrialists and City people: it was seen as the harbinger of more inter-company discrimination to come.

CONTRADICTIONS AND CONFLICTING POLICIES

Political sophisticates may accept that governments sometimes have to pursue conflicting objectives, but among ordinary people apparent contradictions tend to breed bewilderment and cynicism. It is, perhaps, an inescapable consequence of interventionist policies that anomalies and conflicts seem to proliferate. The more visibly active a government is, the more contradictions are likely to show.

During the period 1964-68, critics have claimed to see a number of continuing conflicts in overall policy or professed aims. Examples include the apparent contradiction between the loudly proclaimed objective of faster economic growth and the realities of the balance of payments, highlighted by the appearance of Mr George Brown's National Plan in the autumn of 1965, its use as an election prop in March 1966, and then its obvious abandonment in the 'freeze' of July that year. Another apparent anomaly was the use of the complicated apparatus of Prices and Incomes Policy during 1968 to prevent consumer price rises at a time when the overall economic strategy was to 'squeeze' consumers' expenditure by allowing prices to rise.

When these overall policy contradictions are translated into terms of intervention into individual industries, they tend to cause bewilderment, cynicism, and derision. Consider, for example, the situation of the brewing industry in 1968. The major brewery groups were anxious throughout the year to raise the price of beer by 1d. a pint to offset substantial rises in the costs of production, distribution, and the maintenance of premises. The Government was (apparently) equally anxious to maintain the existing price and used all its powers and blandishments to stop the brewers from recouping cost increases by raising public bar prices. Mrs Barbara Castle, the Minister for Employment and Productivity, was publicly and proudly proclaiming to trade unionists in September that the Government had kept down the price of beer. The claim was, however, short-lived. On 22 November the Chancellor of the Exchequer unceremoniously slapped 1d. a pint extra tax on beer as part of his 'mini-budget' and this, of course, was passed on to the consumer.

Another example of apparently crass contradictions in Government policy comes from the road haulage industry. This industry was the first to be investigated by the National Board for Prices and Incomes in 1965. It has been under virtually continuous review ever since, with batches of recommendations, and exhortations to increase productivity and keep down charges appearing at regular intervals. It may well be the case, of course, that there is merit in these recommendations and, since road haulage charges form part of the costs of all Britain's production for both home and export markets nobody could deny their importance to the economy. Yet the Government has imposed tax and cost increases—via fuel excise duties, road tax, and the cost of the SET forced loan—on the road haulage industry of some £150 million during its term of office. This is far more than the industry could reasonably hope to recoup by any increase in productivity, and further cost rises are presaged by the provisions of the 1968 Transport Act.

Inevitably, these Government actions have led to escalating haulage charges which must have raised costs throughout British industry and commerce. It must have been clearly apparent to the Government's advisers that such effects would occur.

One of the points that arises from these two examples (and of many others resulting from the Prices and Incomes Policy) is the existence of double standards, the obvious belief by politicians that price increases sought by private industry are suspect, whereas those they themselves impose are somehow virtuous or at least patently necessary. Industrialists would hardly be human if they did not find this kind of 'double think' irritating. In more practical terms, they would argue that if anyone should benefit from price rises it should be industry (with potential advantages to investment) and not the ever-open maw of the Treasury.

FORM-FILLING

Enough has probably been said to suggest that accusations of mounting bureaucracy since October 1964, can be substantiated. On most commonsense criteria—the need to notify or seek approval, multiplication of discretionary powers and departments and agencies entitled to intervene, creation of new offences, deliberate and coincidental discrimination between industries and companies, anomalies and contradictions in policies and practices—the hallmarks of the highly centralised society have proliferated swiftly over a four-year period.

Those with an ideological commitment to intervention may argue that such a development is of relatively little importance compared with the anticipated benefits. The less committed are entitled to enquire to what extent the general disadvantages of escalating bureaucracy might outweigh the benefits of intervention, even if it should achieve all the specific hopes of its sponsors.

Some of the disadvantages of bureaucracy are immediately practical. It consumes management and staff time in form-filling, correspondence, and consultation. It consumes management and professional services as companies try to thread their way through the tortuosities of new schemes and laws.

Relatively little is known about the amount of time industry has to spend in compiling official returns and answering questionnaires, though at the time of writing the Confederation of British Industry is conducting a survey among its Scottish members which should shed detailed light on this particular aspect of the bureaucratic burden. There are, however, some published statements by individual companies which give some idea of the orders of magnitude that are involved, and of the way they are increasing.

In 1966 Courtaulds informed a House of Commons Estimates Committee that it had to employ eight men full-time answering official forms. A survey carried out by the Building Department of University College, London, in 1967 quoted one (anonymous) company's estimate that it had to devote 559 man-days a year to completing twenty-seven different forms to be returned annually quarterly and monthly to statutory bodies. A single form, the Ministry of Building and Public Works' annual employment return, required 150 man-days to complete. A second company, when asked to check these calculations, stated that the estimate of man-days required was too low.

Initial results of the CBI's Scottish survey showed that one-third of the respondents received up to twenty-five requests for information during the three-month period July to September 1968; the remainder received between twenty-five and seventy-five forms. Three-quarters of these forms came from Government departments.

The best documented study of the impact of form-filling on an individual company was published in December 1968, by Aims of Industry.* It gave a detailed breakdown of the Government returns which a Chichester based engineering company Wingard Ltd, was required to complete during 1968 (reproduced in the table on pp. 150 and 151). Several points emerge from this particular study. One is the actual total of working days—801—involved in mandatory form filling, equivalent to the full-time employment of three people in a medium-sized company with 770 employees. In effect, 0·39 per cent of all the company's activity is compulsory form-filling. This may not sound especially damaging, but if the Wingard experience is charac-teristic of the situation in British industry as a whole it would imply that around 44,000 people have to be employed simply to make statutory returns. If this volume of effort could be diverted to industrial production, the gain to the nation would be around £130 million per annum!

Another point which emerges from the Wingard study is the extent to which mandatory form-filling is escalating. No less than 769 of the estimated 801 working days had to be devoted to returns which

* *A Case for a Tax Refund to Industry*, Aims of Industry, 1968.

were new to this company in 1968. Not all these returns were the result of interventionist measures taken by the Labour Government; the industry training boards set up under the Conservatives' 1964 Industrial Training Act are prolific generators of paper work, while about a quarter of Wingard's 1968 form-filling burden derived from the quinquennial Census of Production held in that year. But Wingard's chief accountant contrasts the former Income Tax investment allowance, which required one man-hour a year, with Labour's investment grants requiring eighty man days a year, and comments; *Extensive additional work for a negligible cash flow advantage in the long-term.*

There is a genuine dilemma for governments in the form-filling they ask industry to undertake. Insufficient collection of information will result in inadequate industrial and economic statistics (a frequent complaint in Britain) and it may lead to formulation of Government policy from a base of incomplete information. It would therefore not be unreasonable to expect some increase over the years in the returns demanded from companies as attempts are made to improve the published statistics. What companies ought to be able to expect in return is great care on the part of the authorities to ensure a minimum of duplication and overlapping in the collection of statistical material.

Such care had certainly not been shown up to the end of 1968. Instead, the plethora of ministries and agencies empowered by the Labour Government to deal with industry must have made it virtually certain that overlapping and duplication would occur. Some relief may follow from the reforms of statistical services, and especially the setting up of the Business Statistics Office, announced by the Government in 1968, though any noticeable benefits are likely to be slow in emerging.

It would be unduly charitable, in any case, to imply that most of industry's complaints about increasing form-filling stem only from the Government's zeal to provide adequate statistical services. There can be no doubt of the direct link between intervention by Government departments and agencies and proliferating forms. The Industrial Training Act, the 1965 tax 'reforms', the National Plan, investment grants, and SET have all been fruitful generators of routine paperwork. One point to be borne in mind is that many of the Government's so-called 'handouts' to industry are in fact repayments or redistributions of sums already collected in taxes, levies or forced loans. Such processes seem inevitably administratively cumbersome with an appreciable part of the theoretically available benefits swallowed up in executive and clerical costs in both industry and government departments or statutory agencies.

WINGARD LIMITED AND ASSOCIATED COMPANIES
SCHEDULE OF GOVERNMENT STATISTICAL RETURNS

Government department and title of form	Form ref. no.	Frequency	Time taken	Annual working days 1968 (260 working days = 1 year)	Notes
DEPARTMENT OF EMPLOYMENT AND PRODUCTIVITY Monthly Return of Total Wages and Salaries	WS 32	Monthly	½ hour	1	
Numbers Employed and Engaged, Details of Short-time and Overtime	L 2	Monthly	½ day	6	
Earnings of Administrative, Technical and Clerical Staff	SL 65	Annually	1 day	1	
*Analysis by occupation of numbers in employment in manufacturing industries on a given date	L 74	*Not known	5 days	*5	New (to Wingard) return
*Survey of Labour Cost—1968 Cumulative hours/ days/values Cumulative average of numbers	LC 68	*Not known	3 days every week + 20 days summary and analysis	*166	Very complicated headings requiring extensive re-analysis of payroll and accounting information
Analysis of NHI Cards held for each 'establishment'	ED 205	Quarterly	1 day	4	
*Schedule of NHI Cards in respect of persons employed outside districts	ED 920A	Quarterly	2 days	*8	
Accident Frequency Rate	509 a	Annually	3 days	3	
BOARD OF TRADE *Census of Production—1968	—	Every 5 years	1 full-time clerk + 20 days	*280	Extensive analysis by measure and value of purchases and sales over several hundred headings. Re-analysis of purchasing and accounting information
*Investment Grants claims—superseding Income Tax Investment Allowance which required one man-hour a year		Quarterly / Annually	days per period 5 days per qtr. 8 days per annum	*80	Extensive additional work for a negligible cash flow advantage in the long term. Complication of tool sales to customers. Increased analysis/ identification of tooling expense on continuous basis

MINISTRY OF TECHNOLOGY Road Vehicle Components—Total deliveries and exports	—	Monthly	$\frac{1}{2}$ hour	1	
INDUSTRIAL TRAINING BOARDS *Return of number employed, wages and salaries paid	S 1	Annually	2 days	*2	
*Claim for General Grant—including record of training	S 2/S 3	Annually	20 days	*20	*Extensive information*
*Claim for Special Grant					
*Training Registers	—	Continuous	days per week	*104	
*Job Specification Sheet	—	Continuous	days per week	*104	
MINISTRY OF POWER Return of Consumer's receipts, use and stock of steel	C 1 19/1	Quarterly	4 days	16	

*New return in last three or four years.

WINGARD LIMITED AND ASSOCIATED COMPANIES
SCHEDULE OF GOVERNMENT RETURNS ARISING FROM ROUTINE PAYROLL PROCEDURES,
ETC.

	Frequency	Time taken above normal weekly procedure	Annual working days 1968	Notes
PAYROLL PAYE and GRADUATED PENSION—Annual return	Annually	several weeks	45	
NHI—Quarterly return—(in lieu of adhesive stamps or frankings)	Quarterly	2 days	8	
*Selective Employment Tax—Quarterly claim for refund/premium	Quarterly	2–3 days	10	
*Enquiries arising from employees joining, leaving or sick	Continuous			*Considerable increase of work arising from wage-related benefits scheme*
*Contracts of Employment	Continuous	1 day weekly	52	
*Redundancy Payments	(not currently applicable)			
MISCELLANEOUS Purchase Tax	Quarterly	$\frac{1}{2}$ day	2	
Hydrocarbon Oil Rebate	Annually	$\frac{1}{2}$ day $\frac{1}{2}$ day	1	*Accounts Department Supplies Department*
*Export Rebate	Quarterly	2 days	now ceased	

* New return in last three or four years.

SPECIAL INVESTIGATIONS

What has been elaborated so far simply concerns the burden of routine provision of information to Government departments and agencies.

If a company has the misfortune to become involved in the numerous special investigations of bodies like the National Board for Prices and Incomes, the Monopolies Commission or the enquiries of *ad hoc* bodies like the Sainsbury Committee (on the drugs industry) or the Plowden Committee (on the aircraft industry), then the burden of information-giving rises enormously. Moreover, the management level at which this burden must be carried rises to the top echelons of the company.

Few authenticated estimates of the time and money involved for companies in industries investigated by the Prices and Incomes Board have been published. So far as Monopolies Commission investigations are concerned, Osram-GEC has estimated that its involvement in the enquiry into the electric lamp industry cost around £20,000. While other companies have not published figures, enquiries among a number of big companies who have been involved in Monopolies Committees investigations suggest that this estimate is not untypical and may well be decidedly conservative in some cases.

Involvement in major investigations of this kind often entails at least four separate kinds of effort. First, there is a big statistical exercise to provide the investigating body with the basic factual information it requires. The second phase is normally a face-to-face meeting between the company concerned and the investigating body or its consultants. Preparation for this type of meeting normally involves top management and a variety of specialists and professional advisers so that authoritative amplification of information presented can be given and so that the viewpoint of the company on the issues at stake can be put. The third stage is normally one of further consultation and presentation of more detailed information as companies are given the opportunity to react to or comment upon the various alternative courses of action the investigating body may be considering. The final stage, which may be spread over a long period follows the report of the investigating body when consultations with the Government department concerned are the usual outcome.

Special legislation affecting a particular industry or type of activity, can be an equally big consumer of management and specialist time. Substantial consultation between companies and Government departments may well precede the introduction of the legislation. Once it is clear that new measures are passing into law there is likely to be a massive involvement of management time in the consideration and implementation of policy changes resulting from the new legislation. One example of this kind of involvement was given by Mr Henry Lazell, the Chairman of Beechams:*

Increasing intervention means that senior executives are having to spend more and more of their time in examining the implications of legislation and regulations, both existing and proposed, and in dealing with other requirements of Government departments and committees. The damage caused by this diversion of effort to deal with the flow of paper from Whitehall cannot be precisely calculated, but I can give some examples of its effect on our business. For some two years the Executive Vice-Chairman had to devote nearly half his time to matters connected with the Sainsbury Committee's investigations. Had he not been so occupied, he could have assumed responsibility for our European operations at a much earlier date and our affairs in that area would have benefited accordingly. Our Research Director has to spend at least twenty-five per cent of his time dealing with the mounting flow of legislation and regulations affecting our products. Some twenty per cent of the effort of the two UK Divisional Chairmen is taken up in this way and many other senior executives are affected. These men need to devote their energies to promoting the growth of the business. They object very strongly to having their efforts diverted while, at the same time, they are exhorted by the Government to do better.

One of the features of Government intervention generally, and particularly of special investigations which may substantially affect the company's future, is not only the direct involvement of management time in the provision of information or views. On these major matters it is vitally important for companies to appraise the situation in the most detailed manner and there is consequently a major time involvement in preparation within the company of information, in inter-management consultation, and in consultation with specialist advisers. Responsibility for such matters, as Mr Lazell's comments imply, cannot be pushed down the line to relatively junior managers, but is an inevitable consumer of top management time.

CONSULTATION

One of the striking features of the growth of intervention has been the extent to which industrialists have become involved in consultation with government departments and agencies. This is often regarded as a virtue. If the Government is to intervene increasingly in industry it is desirable that such intervention should be made on the basis of the fullest provision of information and of interchange of views between industry, Ministers and civil servants. Consultation

* Beecham Group Ltd, Annual Report 1968.

should, it is argued, avoid the possibility of governments making mistakes in the measures they choose, and should give industry the chance of ensuring that government intervenes in the way which will bring it maximum benefit. To some extent, at least, this view has been endorsed both in theory and in practice by industry itself. Mr John Davies of the Confederation of British Industry, has called for 'partnership' between industry and Government and the most bitter disputes between the CBI and the Government have usually hinged on allegations of inadequate consultation. The extent to which businessmen have allowed themselves to be persuaded into serving on various consultative bodies, or in taking part in the management of an agency of intervention, superficially indicates a readiness to be involved in the process of Government–industry consultation.

In the next chapter we discuss the extent to which Government–industry consultation can ever be really effective and whether 'partnership' with an interventionist government can ever be a practicable proposition. Our concern here is with the narrower issue of the time involvement which a proliferation of consultative and interventionist bodies has placed upon senior industrial personnel.

Management Today (December 1968) succinctly summarised the basic problem in an editorial:

The senior industrialist has a frightening range of Governmental and Government-sponsored organisations clamouring for his attention in the quest for higher national productivity. The DEA, Mrs Castle's transmogrified Ministry, the BNEC, Neddy and all the Little Neddies, the Monopolies Commission, the Training Boards, the PIB, the IRC— the apparatus for purposeful intervention in industry is so complex that its purposes could well be negated by over-lapping. Most of these bodies, after all, are competing for exactly the same men, as 'industrial advisers', or as board members, or as expert witnesses.

This article went on to point out the problem facing the individual manager:

In the last resort, a manager always has his own form of sanction where voluntary groups are concerned. If he finds them (relatively or absolutely) a waste of time, he can always stay away. But you cannot stay away from Government. Not only is it often difficult for a manager to refuse a Whitehall invitation to sit on this committee or that, but even if he does, the body concerned will be after him or his company for information and assistance. H. G. Lazell of the Beecham Group is surely not alone in experiencing an enormous increase in the demands of Government on managerial time in the private sector.

It is not only, however, the demands of Government departments and agencies for the services of senior managers in consultative, advisory or management capacities which constitute the time burden of intervention on senior management. Processes such as 'sponsorship' of industries by departments such as the Ministry of Technology and the Board of Trade impose a further consultative burden upon top managers. It was estimated, at one time, that top managers in the aircraft industry were spending one day in five in consultations with the Government. In those industries in which the Ministry of Technology takes a particular interest, one of the most usual explanations for the absence of a Company Chairman or Managing Director is that he has gone to the Ministry for consultations!

As has already been mentioned it is difficult to fault the basic intentions of this plethora of consultation. Yet it poses a problem of enormous practical importance. Almost by definition, good senior managers are one of the nation's most valuable and scarce resources. It is difficult to believe that substantial absence from their companies, while they are engaged in this kind of consultative and advisory process, does not have some kind of adverse effect upon the efficiency or potential growth of the companies concerned. If the sum of these adverse effects is appreciable, there seems a strong likelihood that the cost to the nation of all this consultation is at least as great as the potential benefits which may be expected from measures of intervention.

One factor in this big burden upon Britain's industrial firms is unquestionably the enormous proliferation of departments, interventionist and consultative bodies—many of them appearing to have a substantial overlap in function and often competing for the same people. This clearly implies that one way of reducing the burden of consultation is to end the proliferation and to make a start upon reducing and rationalising those bodies which already exist.

The fundamental issue, however, goes beyond the question of simply reducing the number of interventionist and consultative agencies. The implication is that every measure of intervention, actual or contemplated, has a definite and potentially high cost in consultative time. This is surely a reasonable indication for caution in producing still more ideas for intervention which are going to impose yet more consultative burdens on senior management.

Another point to be borne in mind is that the time involvement of senior managers is only the visible tip of the consultation iceberg. In many cases the involvement of one senior industrialist also means that he has to employ some of the time of substantial numbers of staff within his company on statistical exercises, preparation of information, examination of alternative possibilities and so on, so that the advice he can offer in his consultative capacity can be of the highest possible level. The people thus employed are themselves of considerable value in their own company jobs and the diversion of their time to the consultative process adds up to another substantial additional cost of intervention. One critic* has claimed that: *'Every addition to the Civil Service in certain higher grades, it should not be forgotten, involves an equivalent amount of extra work for the staff of private firms dealing with the Government Departments concerned, in the shape of clerical workers, tax experts, accountants and so on.'* This may well be a sweeping claim but it does highlight an apparently inevitable consequence of interventionist measures and philosophies whose scale and cost is much too large and serious to be ignored.

PSYCHOLOGICAL EFFECTS

The evidence so far considered substantiates, beyond much reasonable doubt, criticisms that interventionist measures undertaken in Britain during the sixties have led to a significant growth in bureaucracy. We have endeavoured to evaluate some of the practical effects and seen that the cost is high in terms of time wasting among all levels of business staff and in provision for a very substantial increase in civil servants.

Apart from this very real burden in terms of cost and diversion of effort to dubiously productive purposes, a major criticism of the effects flowing from increasing intervention relates to the alleged psychological results. These are inevitably more difficult to pin-point than directly factual matters of money and time involvement. However, the prospective psychological effects of an interventionist climate are so frequently stressed by critics that no evaluation of the effects of intervention can omit at least an attempt to assess the credibility of the criticisms. The alleged psychological effects of intervention fall into three main groups. First, it is suggested, growing intervention produces an atmosphere of uncertainty which saps confidence and diminishes initiative and enterprise. The second group of criticisms suggests that the effects on confidence and enterprise are strongly supplemented by a reduction of incentives. These criticisms particularly relate to interventionist measures in the tax field. The third group of criticisms suggests that increasing intervention produces a general atmosphere of frustration which gives rise to 'fight or flight' reactions. Those who can conveniently do so, withdraw either by physical emigration or deliberate reduction of effort. Those who must stay become increasingly bloody-minded.

* F. Knox, *The Growth of Central Government Manpower*, Aims of Industry Study No. 21, 1968.

By their very nature, factors like confidence and enterprise are almost impossible to measure. There is, however, one relationship which is well established by economic tradition—the link between confidence and private industry investment. We have already traced (Chapters 8 and 12) the disappointing course of private sector industry investment, and particularly of manufacturing investment, during the sixties, with fixed investment in manufacturing in 1967 below the peak it reached as long ago as 1961. As has already been indicated it is difficult to separate the role of industrial intervention in this disappointing record from the generally poor progress of the economy. It has been noted, however, that one of the general effects of the rising tide of intervention has been the creation of growing uncertainty among businessmen. Given such uncertainty the businessman plays safe by avoiding risk investment and it is difficult to believe that this uncertainty factor has not played its part in the investment record. The vogue for take-overs and mergers almost certainly indicates the same lack of confidence. Whereas new capital investment adds to capacity and competition, take-over of existing assets and markets offers a safer alternative.

Lack of incentive must, in common sense, reinforce the disinclination to take risks. This applies with obvious force to the small company where ownership and management are combined. If such companies are to take risks in expansion they must not only feel that economic prospects are worthwhile, that their plans will not be negated by some new and unexpected intervention by the State, but also that they will be permitted to earn and retain rewards commensurate with the risks. It is in this field that Britain's tax system, and particularly the discriminatory 'close company' regulations, bear most heavily. Equally the small businessman is traditionally an individualist whose satisfactions derive not only from making profits but from running his own show in his own way. A climate of intervention, forcing such people into policies and measures selected by the distant hand of Whitehall, can in itself be a strong disincentive.

It is not only, however, among small businesses that one can expect to observe the confidence and disincentive effects of intervention. For most people in middle and senior management in big companies further personal progress depends at least on not involving the company in losses and preferably, of course, in increasing profits. Given a climate of uncertainty or the possibility that potentially profitable projects will be vitiated by some further batch of interventionist measures, the influence of such people will naturally be directed towards the avoidance of risk. Disincentive will again reinforce this tendency, for high surtax levels and the destruction of stock options has made it virtually impossible for companies to offer adequate financial incentives to the successful executive, as many studies have testified.

These considerations suggest that the psychological effects of increasing intervention may well have played a quite significant part in the stagnation of capital investment. There are also reasonable grounds for presuming that they have engendered caution which has impeded the promised 'technical revolution'. Companies simply do not commit themselves to advanced and speculative technology unless they have confidence in general economic prospects, reasonable freedom from interference in pursuing their plans, and some prospect of reaping extra rewards for extra risks.

A variety of phenomena, ranging from student violence to disillusion with politicians has been attributed to 'over Government' and particularly, of course, to the plethora of legislation, regulation and intervention which has failed to produce the promised success in economic and other terms. This is, of course, a conveniently sweeping form of generalisation both for political opponents of the Labour Government and for those who oppose intervention. While it is extremely difficult to select any single factor as unquestionably attributable to frustration caused by the growing tide of intervention, a number of psychologists have suggested mechanisms through which such frustration occurs and manifests itself. An interesting short essay on this topic, by Professor Richard Lynn, was published in 1967.* The essential argument is that intervention, however well intentioned, frustrates the 'achievement drive'. This frustration leads to three common reactions, retreat, escape and counter-attack. The businessman's 'retreat' is not to put his full efforts into his work. His 'escape' may be either emigration (2,000 British managers emigrated during 1966) or away from the uncertainties and hazards of running a business into salaried employment. 'Counter-attack' by businessmen is perhaps not especially evident, but increasing subscriptions to political and other organisations hostile to increasing State intervention may be regarded as one form of fighting back.

Professor Lynn suggests that counter-attack is now clearly evident within the trade union movement:

It is interesting to observe that now the trade unions are being bossed by the Prices and Incomes Board, in so far as they are being told that they cannot have wage increases they too are counter-attacking this increase in State power, even though it is being introduced by a government of their own party and supposedly for their

* Richard Lynn, 'National Planning and Industrial Frustration', published in *Growth Through Industry*, Institute of Economic Affairs, 1967.

own good. The frustration of achievement drives puts a severe strain on traditional friendships.

PERSONAL FREEDOM

The growth of bureaucracy, as described earlier, represents a very substantial erosion of the freedom of the businessman or industrial executive to run his business in the way he judges to be most profitable. He faces a substantial new series of controls, prohibitions, complexities and penalties with a host of new regulatory agencies empowered to intervene.

It would no doubt be unduly dogmatic to condemn all that has happened in the last decade simply on the grounds that it represents a considerable erosion of personal freedom. Advances such as the Factories Acts, which we now take for granted, were at the time of their introduction attacked as gross interference with the liberty of the businessman, but nobody would today argue for their repeal. It has, however, for long been an article of faith in democratic countries' resistance to authoritarian systems that free men work better and more efficiently than those subject to massive control and regulation. If this is true, there is clearly scope for a good deal of speculation on how far the increase in controls and Governmental pressures on businessmen has inhibited the effort and drive for efficiency which one should, at least in theory, expect from free enterprise industry.

CAREER PROSPECTS FOR THE YOUNG EXECUTIVE

Many industrialists have drawn attention to difficulties in attracting good graduates into careers in industry. There are many strands in this problem. Among them are the deliberate policies pursued by successive governments of raising Civil Service and academic salaries to levels competitive with those paid by industry. As was shown in Chapter 9, the high rewards which industry used to be able to provide for the outstandingly successful have been drastically whittled away by the incidence of surtax and capital gains tax and the virtual prohibition of stock options.

It seems probable that the deterrent effects of such processes may be reinforced by the increasing regulation of industry. One of the traditional psychological attractions of a career in industry was that as executives progressed to senior positions they entered a world of action and decision and considerable real personal power. The more industry is regulated, restricted and directed the less effective power the industrial executive possesses. It is not unreasonable to suppose that some potential executives of high calibre and ambition who would gladly contemplate a career devoted to wrestling with purely industrial problems will shrink from the career prospects in an industrial world where management's time is increasingly involved in contacts with bureaucracy.

The same considerations apply with especial force to the potential entrepreneur. Part of his dynamic, as has already been noted, is the freedom traditionally associated with running his own business. The more restrictive the environment in which business operates, the less are the attractions to the entrepreneur. It is difficult to believe that continuation of the present interventionist climate will not lead to further diminution in the already inadequate supply of creative entrepreneurs in British industry.

Some of those with high potential will doubtless emigrate to freer environments. Others will doubtless seek outlets other than business for their energies, while many of those who do enter the business field may well balance effort, risk and reward more carefully than has traditionally been the case with the entrepreneur.

SOME CONCLUSIONS

In attempting to evaluate the psychological effects of growing intervention one inevitably moves into fields of theory and speculation and thence back into the ideological arguments which surround the subject. Those who support State intervention tend simply to accept growing bureaucracy as a worthwhile price to pay for the putative benefits of Governmental attempts to make industry more efficient or more subservient to overall economic policies. They tend to dismiss psychological effects as either non-existent or as something which will disappear in time as industrialists learn to live with increasing intervention. Naturally enough, those who are ideologically opposed to interventionism are also those who most frequently and vigorously draw attention to the growth of bureaucracy, to its practical cost and time wasting consequences and to its psychological effects.

In so far as there can be any common ground between these two extremes, it would appear to lie in the possibility of simplifying measures of industrial intervention and in making them less of an administrative nightmare. There is probably some important scope in this field simply from the application of good management and Organisation and Methods techniques. Amalgamation of some of the existing agencies of intervention and simplification of procedures would make at least a marginal impact on the degree of bureaucracy involved.

Some relatively small changes in philosophy would also bring advantages. One of the complaints of businessmen about the current interventionist climate is frequent lack of a sense of proportion.

The Government's obsession with tax avoidance, the elevation of relatively minor price and wage rises to major issues, demand for massive documentation to obtain small grants or concessions are the kind of matters which make intervention increasingly irksome and irritating to businessmen. It is, of course, an excellent principle that all should be treated equally before the law, but this provides good reason for careful pre-consideration of policies and legislation to ensure that they will not involve use of a huge Government steam hammer to crack very small nuts.

This, of course, brings us back to the fundamental question of the degree of detailed intervention which is either practicable or tolerable. Except, perhaps, to the extreme Left, there must clearly be some point at which detailed intervention becomes self-defeating because of the administrative burdens it imposes and because of the circumscription which it places on individual initiative and effort.

How near to this point has the increase in intervention since 1964 brought us—or has it already taken us beyond the point of diminishing returns?

CHAPTER FOURTEEN

The future of intervention

The Labour Party returned to power in 1964 largely on the hopes it had inspired of faster economic growth. To achieve its narrow electoral victory it had, of course, exploited all the grievances which it believed to exist among voters—the cost of living, housing shortages, regional employment disparities, old age pensions, the education system and the health service featured prominently on the hustings—and it also did not hesitate to appeal to egalitarianism with attacks on alleged 'privilege', 'speculation' and other traditional targets of Socialist hostility. It is unlikely that these appeals would have captured the vital 'floating vote' if they had not been supplemented by credible claims that a Labour government would know how to end 'stop-go' and move the nation forward into an era of steadily increasing prosperity.

There is no reason to doubt that the Party leaders genuinely believed these claims. It had always been an article of faith among even the most moderate elements in the Labour Party that economies could be planned and directed and controlled into growth and affluence and, as usual, there was no lack of Socialist academic economists articulate with theories on how the trick could be done. Moreover, the essential features of Labour's economic strategy—indicative planning, incomes policy, encouragement of capital investment and technology—were not matters of current controversy. They had all been embraced by the Conservative Party and largely endorsed by the industrial Establishment, the old Federation of British Industries. Instead of having to defend itself against charges of intending interference in complicated industrial matters it did not understand, the Labour Party at the 1964 General Election enjoyed the unusual luxury of being the most credible exponent of what were virtually consensus policies.

This is an important point, for it means that Labour began its experiments in interventionist economics in as near an ideal psychological climate as any government in a democracy can reasonably hope for. There was ample goodwill on both sides of industry, and support for the general strategy promised by Labour from a wide range of political opinion. Of course, the incoming Labour Administration inherited a baleful economic situation, which could justifiably be regarded as delaying the achievement of some of the promised objectives—but not as an excuse for the uninterrupted series of disasters which have characterised 1964–68.

THE INTERVENTIONISTS' DILEMMA

When, in Chapter 8, we surveyed the years of disillusionment which have followed the high hopes of 1964, we suggested that Labour had hopelessly overrated the beneficial effects which industrial intervention can achieve in a free society. (The same charges can, of course, be laid against the many non-Socialist intellectuals who made such a vogue of economic planning during the early sixties.) Nothing we have uncovered in our more detailed survey of the effects of Labour's interventionist measures (Chapters 9 to 13) need cause any revision of this thesis.

We saw that regional policies and attempts to promote the 'technical revolution' have absorbed resources which were substantial by British standards, but produced quite minimal discernible results. The Kaldor theories on how to promote capital investment through the tax system have been applied in an agonising spasm of 'reform', and supplemented by new non-profits-related grants: industrial investment stagnated, in real terms, at 1961 levels during the years 1965–68. 'Industrial restructuring' has largely consisted of a virtually uncontrolled wave of mergers and takeovers which owed little to 'industrial logic' or Government agencies, but a good deal to continuous deflation and some unexpected side-effects of the tax 'reforms'. Four years of feverish bureaucratic activity on Incomes Policy have produced earnings levels broadly equal to those which theory would have predicted *in the absence* of Incomes Policy.

All these examples can be regarded as exploding the theory that there are a relatively limited number of simplistic actions which governments need only take to cure the ills of a complex industrial economy. What they suggest is that, to achieve any intended effect, intervention has to take place on a much vaster scale than anything the Labour Government has contemplated during the period 1964–68. If this is a correct assumption, it poses a dilemma: really large-scale intervention in terms of financial resources would inevitably produce major economic distortions, while large-scale intervention via extensive detailed controls would (see Chapter 13) probably be self-defeating because of its psychological and disincentive effects.

POTENTIAL SMALL BENEFITS

If this basic dilemma has been correctly described, it means that state intervention in industry can never transform an economy in the speedy and beneficial manner which Socialists have long claimed to be possible. It does not, however, preclude the possibility that intervention on a scale possible in a reasonably free society may produce enough benefits (and few enough disadvantages) to be worthwhile.

In our survey of the effects of Labour's interventionist measures (Chapters 9 to 13) we noted a number of apparent small-scale successes. It was suggested, for example, that the pre-production orders and subsidised trials schemes for advanced machine tools had made a useful, if modest contribution to the advance of engineering technology in Britain. Some of the Production Advisory Services of the Ministry of Technology have produced beneficial results at relatively small cost, while the work of the National Computing Centre and some of the other Mintech measures to promote the use of computers in Britain have made modest contributions to either the scope or efficiency of application of these advanced aids to management. Redundancy payments and more generous unemployment benefits have probably had at least marginally useful results in reducing resistance to change.

There are doubtless other examples of measures of intervention which have been unequivocally beneficial. Much more common, however, are examples where benefits have accrued but have been offset by unwelcome side effects. The battery of measures used to promote Labour's regional policies have had some marginal effects in reducing regional employment disparities, but they have produced some damaging economic distortions in the process. In particular, highly restrictive use of industrial development certificates has forced some new projects into Development Areas, while causing a good deal of projected (and probably urgently needed) investment to be abandoned or deferred.

Similarly, Incomes Policy has had some beneficial effects in bringing productivity considerations into wage negotiations and stimulating the spread of productivity bargaining in Britain. The cost, however, in bureaucratic processes, unacceptable restrictions on traditional liberties, and consequent psychological 'backlash' has been so high as to make the whole effort counter-productive.

By analysing the genuinely successful examples of Labour's interventionist measures and comparing them with the partial and outright failures one can pass some tentative judgments on the scope for beneficial intervention in the British economy.

SOME CRITERIA FOR SUCCESSFUL INTERVENTION

Some obvious characteristics emerge from the examples of successful intervention. First, they are mostly schemes with limited and severely practical objectives. Few of them are grandiose attempts to achieve 'revolutions' or 'miracles'. In terms of resources employed, or of initial changes in the methods or policies of the companies affected by them, their scope has been modest.

Second, they have been genuinely co-operative efforts between Government and industry. They have been designed to meet needs diagnosed or acknowledged by industrialists, not to conform to somebody's economic theories. They have been wholly voluntary and non-discriminatory in operation, with companies free, within the terms of the schemes, to participate or not at will.

Third, their operation has been kept simple and entrusted largely to practical people with experience in the fields concerned. Little scope has been left for the discretion or discrimination of politicians and civil servants.

As might be expected, the measures of intervention which have been dubiously successful or disastrously damaging to the economy have shown most of the opposite characteristics of those schemes which have been successful. The biggest failures have been the most grandiose attempts at intervention—the attempts to force industry into higher capital investment through discriminatory taxation or to hold back earnings through Incomes Policy. The unsuccessful schemes have also usually been imposed willy-nilly on unenthusiastic or hostile industrialists, usually with either minimal consultation or the type of discussions in which the Government has listened to industry's objections and taken no notice of them. Such measures have usually been aimed at remedying some alleged malady diagnosed in some Whitehall backroom, and the prescriptions have born all the hallmarks of total unfamiliarity with the way industry works. Schemes emanating in such conditions are usually immensely complex in operation, employing armies of bureaucrats and giving maximum discretion to politicians and their agents. Characteristically such schemes create damaging uncertainty in industry and involve major elements of discrimination between industries and companies. Such schemes are likely to fail when participation is voluntary; when it is compulsory, they can do major damage to the economy.

LABOUR'S MISTAKES

It has been one of the more unfortunate characteristics of the Labour Government's term of office that it has made relatively little use of small-scale, practical beneficial schemes, and major use of highly theoretical, grandiose, mandatory measures. The unlikelihood of success of these grandiose schemes has unfortunately been compounded by confusion of industrial and doctrinaire political aims. The most obvious example was the notorious tax 'reforms' of 1965. Although it set out with the laudable intention of persuading industry to invest more, the Labour Government could not resist the temptation to combine this aim with a major doctrinaire attack on the investor. Unfortunately for Britain, the extreme socialist theories of Professor Kaldor lay ready to hand and were rushed into effect counter to all the current taxation trends in Europe. Other notorious examples of the translation of socialist prejudice into industrial intervention include the attack on road haulage in the 1968 Transport Act, and the various measures of discrimination against service industries.

Another feature of Labour's interventionist measures which has prejudiced their success and given great scope for doing positive economic damage has been the extent to which schemes which give maximum discretion to politicians or their agents have been introduced. The potential damage is twofold. First, such schemes make a mockery of the rule of law. In such manifestations the Industrial Reorganisation Corporation and the Industrial Expansion Act has given virtually unlimited powers to ministers, or people appointed by them, to intervene wherever or however they like in industry. In so far as there is a saving grace, it lies in the fact that no compulsory powers are wielded, but a virtually limitless supply of Government money provides the next best thing. The existence of such powers, and the scope for their arbitrary use, constitutes a major element of uncertainty for industrialists.

The second danger in interventionist schemes of this type is that ministers or their agents will use them for purposes which are detrimental to the real interests of the economy. Being appointed Minister of Technology or Secretary of State for Economic Affairs does not automatically bring understanding of the complex workings of a modern industrial economy. Nor does the recruitment of a number of eminent industrialists to the board of an organisation like the Industrial Reorganisation Corporation ensure that questions of industrial structure or finance will be better decided than the market forces could have achieved.

The dangers of ministers and interventionist agencies committing themselves to unwise courses of action are little diminished by the rounds of informal, confidential discussions with industrialists which are an increasing feature of Labour's interventionist regime. Anthony Harris, the Economic Editor of the *Guardian*, has suggested that such discussions bring their own hazards:*

* *Guardian*, 11 February 1969.

In intervening directly in industry, the Government inevitably acts more and more informally.

This sounds harmless enough, but it is not. Where there is no declared policy and no formal procedure decisions, however much they may be dressed up with words like 'selective' and with post hoc *explanations, become essentially personal and arbitrary.*

What is worse, a Minister who has it in his power to bestow public backing and public money on what need be little more than a whim is a helpless prey to lobbying.

Also: however much Ministers and their departments may be convinced that they are pursuing nothing but the national good, what real chance have they with no formal powers to call and sift evidence before expert judges, to find the weaknesses in the special pleadings of those who know so much more about the details and special factors of an industrial situation than they do.

Another feature of Labour's intervention in industry has been frequent attempts to combine social and industrial objectives. Regional policies constitute an outstanding example, while the emphasis on the lower paid in incomes policy is another. It is, of course, understandable that a government should attempt to bring maximum social benefits with its intervention in industry, while cynics might add that such a policy also helps to secure votes. Generally speaking, however, confusion of social and industrial ends tends to achieve maximum economic inefficiency. Thus regional policy would almost certainly have been more effective in industrial terms if it had pursued the 'growth zone' concept instead of trying to spread new industrial developments thinly over half the United Kingdom. Similarly it seems certain that incomes policy does the nation a disservice if it tends to discourage the acquisition of increased skill or the assumption of increased responsibility.

If British governments are to continue to intervene in industry, then, there are many ways in which they can learn from Labour's mistakes.

They should avoid the grandiose scheme which is supposed to put the economy to rights at the clang of a division bell. They should avoid the administratively complex, which is going to spawn an army of bureaucrats, especially if it is going to involve politicians and civil servants in taking what are basically business decisions. They should shun the tidy theories of academics and be aware that mixing political prejudices (however strongly held) or social objectives (however intrinsically worthy) with intervention is unlikely to augment economic efficiency. Above all, they should not over-estimate the extent to which political intervention can influence industrial progress—except to stop it dead in its tracks.

It would not be difficult to enumerate many other 'don'ts'. Simply to apply the above principles would suggest that much of what has been attempted during our period of study would have been better left undone.

WHAT SHOULD FOLLOW?

If Labour's over-fussy and largely ineffective apparatus of intervention should be substantially dismantled, what, if anything, should take its place? Should industry be largely left to its own devices, as it was during the 1950s and given only the most general kind of direction and persuasion through the relatively clumsy apparatus of overall economic management? Is there scope, perhaps, for the beneficial use of forms of intervention, differing from those which Labour has attempted, or maybe for devising new methods of Government–industry collaboration? Must governments stand by impotently if industry fails to meet the expectations of the electorate? Could any British Government really withdraw from detailed involvement in industry, even if it wanted to?

These are obviously enormously important questions—and highly controversial ones. They are unlikely to be settled definitively, but it is worth looking at some of the courses of action which have been urged over a broad range of the political spectrum, by those who care passionately about the future of British industry and who seek the same ends of more rapid and soundly based economic growth, permanent international competitiveness for the British economy, and steadily rising living standards for our people.

One popular line of argument is that industry and Government must increasingly work more closely together whether or not either side likes the process, and therefore both sides had better get on with working out some objectives, mechanisms, and ground rules. This is to only a limited extent a self-evident proposition. It derives on the one hand from assumed pressures by the electorate on the political parties. It supposes that industrial performance will never live up to national economic expectations of its own accord and that the Government, any Government, must therefore be (and be seen to be) constantly prodding and pushing and helping industry to achieve the level and direction of performance which the national interest is presumed to require. A second strand in this kind of argument derives from a somewhat selective view of what happens overseas. British industry, it is argued, has to compete internationally with industries which receive varying degrees of practical help from their Governments, including such things as relatively 'soft' capital and the rather less tangible benefits of such things as national economic plans. The obverse to this particular argument lies in the fact that at any given time there is usually a fairly substantial number of private-sector British industries and companies receiving or seeking Government help either financially or through some kind of protective arrangement.

A third supporting argument for the 'industry and Government must get closer together' line of thought is that industry will not of its own accord do those things which the pundits regard as plainly desirable in the national interest—or at least it will not do them quickly enough or on a sufficient scale. It will not, for example, achieve a high enough rate of investment unless the Government helps it with finance, or it may invest in less desirable activities unless the Government does something to modify the direction of effort. Similarly industry will not of its own accord help to solve major social problems such as regional unemployment, nor will it restructure itself in the 'right' ways.

In total, this may sound like a pretty formidable case. In fact, in both central principle and in detail, it is far from conclusive. The central principle it relies upon is the concept of an enormously wise and knowledgeable Government which can somehow be relied upon to make the right judgments on what industry ought to be doing and on some limited number of mechanisms which will somehow succeed in giving real help with the enormously diverse and sometimes conflicting needs of a huge spectrum of industries and companies.

So far as the more detailed arguments are concerned, while no one would deny that economic expectations exert enormous electoral pressure, past demands that Governments should do something to improve industrial performance stem to a very considerable degree from the politicians' own propaganda. Both the Conservatives in the early 1960s, and then Labour in the General Election of 1964 and afterwards exaggerated what could be achieved by planning and other forms of Government intervention in industry. Labour, of course, hopelessly oversold the idea of a wise and dynamic Government bringing about a miraculous transformation in industrial performance and is now reaping the harvest of disappointment which could inevitably have been predicted. It seems probable that Labour politicians were misled by their own beliefs (or by the theories of their advisers) into this huge exaggeration of what could be achieved by intervention. In so far as experience to date has not produced the necessary disillusion it is up to the Opposition and other informed commentators to try to re-educate the public on the very restricted limits within which State intervention could be even expected to have any beneficial effects. It is noteworthy that in countries like the United States and West Germany where the fashion for State intervention has never been propagandised by major political parties there is little electoral expectation of Government action to improve industrial performance.

Those who argue for a substantial apparatus of Government–industry collaboration on the analogy of what happens overseas, usually quote the examples of France and Japan. French indicative planning was the admired model on which the NEDC and 1965 National Plans were based. As it happens enthusiasm for national planning appears to be waning in France, while relatively few French industrialists regard the planning exercises as having had any very large part in the national growth rate. The operations of Japan's Ministry of International Trade and Industry (MITI) are also often commended as a model which Britain should follow. MITI covers an extraordinarily wide range, corresponding broadly to our own DEA, Board of Trade, Ministry of Power, and Department of Employment and Productivity—in addition to operating the alcohol monopoly! Like the DEA, MITI carries out detailed national planning exercises, and like the French authorities it can give substantial incentives to industrialists to follow the plan projections by the provision of subsidies, or capital on favourable terms, or special tax concessions. Whatever the merits of the planning systems, one of the distinguishing features about both the French and Japanese types of intervention is the use of State funds to promote particular industrial developments in economies without well-developed capital markets. It is permissible to doubt whether these systems would have developed in their present manner if French and Japanese industrialists had access to the highly developed capital markets of Britain and the United States. This is one reason for doubting whether there is any need for French- or Japanese-type systems here. Another, of course, lies in the fact, rarely mentioned by interventionists, that the achievements of the French and Japanese have been surpassed by those of West Germany, which has stood rigorously aloof from State intervention in industry. Similarly the world's richest nation, the United States, has arrived at that position entirely through the operation of free market forces.

The success of West German and American industry inevitably causes one to doubt the argument that left to themselves industrialists do not invest enough or export enough, or otherwise behave in the ways which Governments would wish. There would appear to be a strong case for at least as careful study to be given to the free market elements which have induced this kind of industrial achievement in Germany and America, as is so admiringly given to the French and Japanese examples.

NEW FORMS OF COLLABORATION
There is a spectrum of intelligent modern opinion which sees Government–industry collaboration as avoidance of the grosser

forms of State intervention, but instead as a kind of eminently
reasonable mutual help. John Davies, the Director General of the
Confederation of British Industry has called for 'partnership'*
between Government and industry. Michael Shanks has advocated
the 'quasi contract'.† Even the Prime Minister spoke glowingly
about the first National Productivity Conference as a 'parliament
of industry', though this particular 'parliament' met only once more
and was then abandoned by a kind of tacit mutual consent.

The underlying sentiment in ideas of this kind is, of course,
attractive enough. Government and industry are both composed
largely of reasonable men with broad aims in common and they
ought therefore to be able to meet together and devise ways of
giving substantial help to each other.

The deceptive thing about this line of argument is that it over-
looks, or at least under-estimates, a massive degree of short term
incompatibility in both the aims and methods of Government and
industrialists. There is no long term incompatibility, for the sum of
the total distant objectives of industrialists are almost certain to add
up to a state which is desirable to any kind of Government. Within
the short term objectives, however, there are likely to be a whole
array of short term incompatibilities. This arises because industry
must inevitably operate at the level of the individual company. The
essence of the competitive system is that the companies in each
individual industry should pursue objectives which have a considerable degree of incompatibility with each other. They must do battle
with each other for finite markets growing at a limited rate. They
must back differing judgments about the likely course of technical
development, consumer preference, the most efficient types of
process, and hundreds of other matters.

This pursuit of conflicting objectives by competitive means
constitutes the market economy, which has proved by far the most
efficient and productive mechanism for increasing national and
world material well-being. Its inevitable implication, however, is
that there is no such thing as 'Industry' in the sense of some homogeneous body which can enter into partnership with another genuinely homogeneous body, the Government. There are, of course,
matters of common industrial concern on which a broadly repre-
sentative body like the Confederation of British Industry can offer
views which represent what a majority of industrialists are thinking.
The more interventionist the Government in power is, the more
frequently such views will have to be put forward in the hope of

* 'Industry and Government,' George Earle Memorial Lecture, 1966 (Industrial
Educational and Research Foundation, London).
† *The Times*, 25 November 1968.

either securing the abandonment of some proposed intervention as positively harmful, or securing the modification of features which are likely to damage the interests of a majority of companies. Even in such cases the views put forward by the CBI may well be compromises, a kind of highest common factor among the conflicting interests of thousands of companies constituting the membership.

The 'partnership' concept becomes even more difficult when one moves down to the level of individual industries, for here one is dealing with companies in direct competition with each other. There are again a few matters of common concern on which the industry can speak as a reasonably unified whole through the trade association or 'little Neddy'. There is no difficulty, for example, in obtaining a concerted motor industry view on the habit of successive Governments of restricting the home market for vehicles every time some economic crisis threatens: they hate it! These unifying, non-competitive causes, however, are relatively rare. They nearly all arise either from State intervention or from alleged lack of necessary action by the Government. Outside these matters, individual industries able to enter into partnership with the Government are as much abstractions as 'Industry'.

Those who want 'partnership' to go beyond this very limited range of non-competitive matters must, in fact, be advocating something suspiciously near to market-sharing. If, for example, the growth of capacity in an industry is to be planned in partnership with the Government, the inevitable implication is that the industrialists concerned must reach some kind of agreement on how the growth of the market is to be divided between them. This is cartelisation, whatever kind of benevolent approval some Government department may give it. Beyond a few obvious matters of common concern on which members of an industry may properly unite to 'lobby' the Government it is difficult to see scope for partnership between industry and Government which is not destructive of the market economy.

'QUASI CONTRACTS'

Much the same objections apply to the concept of 'quasi contracts', a form of company–Government collaboration which has been considerably used in Japan and France and is also not unknown in Britain (although when it occurs it is not normally acknowledged as such). The essence of a 'quasi contract' is that a company reaches an agreement with the Government to establish some venture or process or adopt some course of action which the Government regards as desirable in the national interest. In return the Government makes some concession to the company. 'Quasi contracts' have been used to a certain extent in France to promote regional balance, with companies agreeing to set up factories in particular areas in exchange for concessions such as capital advances or promises of Government contracts. In Japan 'quasi contracts' have been used on a wider scale with inducements such as tax concessions, 'soft' capital or special planning permissions as a reward for pursuing activities regarded as particularly desirable by the Ministry of International Trade and Industry. In Britain we see something approaching the 'quasi contract' concept when mergers undertaken at the behest of the Industrial Reorganisation Corporation are exempted from Monopolies Commission scrutiny. Another example of the 'quasi contract' in Britain was the aluminium smelter arrangements, where the nationalised fuel industries, with the encouragement of the Government, pledged special concessionary prices to make the projects economic.

Some of those who urge more Government–industry collaboration in Britain feel that much more extended use of the 'quasi contract' mechanism would be a suitable instrument. One of its attractions is that, at least in theory, it constitutes a bargain freely entered into by both sides. Another advantage is that of flexibility: the Government can achieve specific ends by a variety of individual acts of collaboration with companies instead of having to force or bribe whole sectors of industry into particular rigid moulds. Each 'quasi contract' can be treated as a small experiment in Government–industry collaboration, to be modified, if the parties wish, at some later date. It can be repeated with other companies if successful, but if it proves a failure its effects will be confined within relatively narrow bounds.

Against these attractions must be set the fact that the use of 'quasi contracts' inevitably leads to serious inequity between companies. 'Quasi contracts' are only open to big companies. Smaller companies are not likely to be able to act on the scale necessary to make a 'quasi contract' an attractive proposition to the Government. Since the essence of the 'quasi contract' idea is that the companies entering into them obtain some advantages which they could not otherwise have achieved, it follows that the use of 'quasi contracts' must increase the advantages of big companies over their smaller competitors. In so far as the concessions given by the Government cost public funds, small companies would effectively be paying taxes to subsidise their big competitors. Inequity between companies in an industry could go beyond increasing imbalance of advantage between large and small companies. In many cases the Government need would only permit one 'quasi contract' in an industry with perhaps half a dozen large companies as possible recipients. The award of the contract would in effect, amount to a Government-given advantage for one company over its competitors. We have already seen that there is an inherent tendency in many forms of intervention to cause arbitrary inequities between companies. A system of 'quasi contracts' would strongly accentuate this process.

These remarks assume that the companies entering into 'quasi contract' did so on the proper basis for profit-making organisations, i.e. that they only accepted the contract because they could make more profit in this way. It is not difficult, however, to envisage circumstances in which governments would attempt to pressurise companies into accepting 'quasi contract' terms which gave them less profit than the course of action they would otherwise have pursued. This would be especially probable with very large companies entering into several 'quasi contracts', when it might be expected that the authorities would try to offset one example giving the company substantial advantages, with another where the company sacrificed some profitability in achieving what the Government required. As with other forms of intervention the 'quasi contract' system rests upon the assumption that governments somehow possess the wisdom to select industrial projects which will be especially good for the national interest. The projects in which they are likely to get involved are almost invariably those which neither industry nor the capital markets will back from their own resources—by definition projects which are of dubious economic value as judged by the tests of the market place. The idea that the Government can some-how select from a range of such projects some winners into which national resources can properly be poured is a good deal lacking in credibility. If projects which would easily go ahead with industries' own resources are taken to the Government, then the most likely reason is that the company concerned hopes to get 'soft' terms. This is almost by definition uneconomic. Alternatively, if the Government intervenes to secure modifications and give concessions in a project which would otherwise go ahead there will at least be grounds for suspicion that it has intervened to turn an otherwise economic project into one of more dubious value.

MAKING UP FOR MANAGEMENT DEFICIENCIES

Many people who favour Government intervention in industry do so on a *faute de mieux* basis. They regard the process as theoretically undesirable, but as essential if industry will not remedy its own alleged defects with sufficient speed and vigour. Sir Richard Powell, a former Permanent Secretary at the Board of Trade, has argued, for example:* *It would therefore be better if industry could do more of its own reconstruction and rationalisation for itself; but if it is to do this it must produce in greater numbers managers with imagination to see what is needed and the initiative and energy to set about doing it. I should therefore like to see still more encouragement given to the young and not so young to educate themselves in management and to develop their talents more vigorously and rapidly. It must obviously take time to produce a general change in outlook, but it would in the longer term be the best and most reliable way to ensure that industry is equipped to make for itself those changes that we all know need to be made. If standards of management could be raised in this way the need for direct intervention by the Government would diminish and a new relationship between industry and Government would grow up. Government could then devote its energies to managing the economy as a whole and to providing an environment within which industry could flourish while industry could tackle its own problems, and be equipped to run its affairs in its own and the nation's interest.*

This line of argument suffers from several defects. It makes the usual State intervention assumption that Government officials or agencies will somehow be possessed of superior wisdom about industrial matters to managers actually involved in industry. That this is a dubious proposition was acknowledged by Sir Richard Powell in the same lecture: *Government cannot know as much in detail about the problems of industry as industry does itself,* he said, *and it is hard for Government to be selective in its actions. There is therefore always a possibility that what it tries to do may not be the right thing, that more money may be spent than is really needed, and that intervention designed to promote greater efficiency may degenerate into action to prop up for political reasons industries which or economic reasons ought to be allowed to decline or perish.* A second defect is the assumption that the Government will possess the judgment and wisdom to decide rightly when the moment has come to reduce or withdraw its intervention. Any form of Government intervention in fact creates vested interests both in Whitehall and in industry. Dismantling an apparatus for intervention, unless it has made itself universally unpopular, is likely to be a matter of considerable controversy.

A third defect in the argument that Governments must intervene to make up for management deficiencies stems from some confusion about the causes and nature of the alleged defects. It is usually assumed that managements do not take the courses of action which the pundits regard as desirable because they lack the imagination

* 'Industry and Government,' George Earle Memorial Lecture, 1968 (Industrial Educational and Research Foundation, London).

or skill or ability to do so. This is doubtless sometimes the case, but it is probably at least as often true that the general economic background that the Government has created provides inadequate incentive or pressure for companies to make major changes in policies, with the risks that this entails. It has already been argued in this book that the disappointing record on both capital investment and technological advance under the Labour Government is not some reprehensible aberration on the part of industrialists, but a quite inevitable reaction to the thoroughly unpropitious climate for risk taking which the Government's policies have created. It is difficult to believe that a Government which fails to create the circumstances in which beneficial activities like capital investment and technological innovation can flourish can through detailed intervention in industry remedy the situation under the guise of putting right the deficiencies of management.

To argue in this way is not to suggest that improvement in the quality of British management is not urgently desirable. It is fatally easy, however, to over-rate the effects of inadequate management training and to under-rate the effects of inadequate management motivation. Industry has a habit of putting matters right of its own accord if survival is at stake or the prospective rewards are worthwhile. It is not unreasonable to suppose that we should hear a good deal less about the alleged deficiencies of British management if a more competitive but more rewarding climate of operations were to be established.

THE BEGGING BOWL OF PRIVATE ENTERPRISE

Not all Government intervention is of course pressed upon unwilling industrialists by interventionist-minded Ministers and civil servants. At any point of time a substantial amount of industrial activity is being carried on under Government financial auspices, and there is a fairly continuous procession of industrialists seeking new Government aid. If this kind of aid is desirable or necessary, it can be argued that there is relatively little that Governments can do to reduce their intervention in industry and they had better continue with a comprehensive involvement in industrial matters so that they are best equipped to discriminate between industry's demands for aid and to prevent too many demands for help arising in the future.

Governments commonly intervene at industry's request on three different grounds. First, they have for long given help to declining industries so as to maintain employment or to resist the threat of increasing imports. A second reason for invited intervention arises when companies or industries wish to proceed with projects which are too expensive for their own resources and which are claimed to be in the national interest: in Britain the aerospace industries have been the major recipients of this kind of help. A third kind of invited intervention has arisen when declining industries have reached the point where reduction in the number of companies involved, or their regrouping, has become necessary and Government funds have been sought to ease the restructuring process.

It is easy enough to see the dilemmas which arise for a well-intentioned Government when it receives approaches from industrialists for help for any of these reasons. No Government wishes to lay itself open to reproaches that it has helped to kill a particular industry or to cause substantial unemployment or to stand idle in face of a flood of imports, or to exclude the nation from participation in some bold and potentially profitable industrial venture. This is particularly the case because particular industries and particular projects develop highly articulate lobbies in Parliament and the Press.

The dilemma is equally acute for industrialists. They can rightly regard themselves as having a duty to their shareholders and their employees to take all possible measure for the survival of their businesses, and this includes approaching the Government for help if it seems even remotely likely. The more often the precedent is set of Government help for an ailing industry, the more likely it becomes that help may be forthcoming for the next deserving case. Declining industries can also always present their case in terms of the national interest. The decline of industries like cotton or coal or paper does inevitably mean rising imports of these or substitute products. It can similarly be argued that Government failure to support some new aerospace or computer programme will lead to increased imports and the loss of potential exports.

Yet another reason for Government finance for industrial projects arises from the growing fashion for international co-operation. While there is nothing to stop a good deal of useful collaboration between companies across international frontiers, many of the projects which are deemed particularly suitable for international collaboration are of the high risk, high cost, type such as Concorde and the European Air-bus, which require Government sponsorship and finance if they are to proceed. As we have seen there is often a political element in the conception of such projects; the companies who get involved in them not unnaturally want terms that eliminate or minimise the risks involved.

On all these grounds one would expect the involvement of Governments at industry's invitation to increase. It can be reasonably predicted that as the pace of technological development continues to increase, more industries will be overtaken by the signs of decline. Equally, advancing technology will mean that more and more high cost, high risk, projects will be put forward as deserving candidates for the financial support of one or more Governments.

This is particularly so because in virtually every case where Government help is sought by industry it is because normal market forces have effectively pronounced an adverse judgment on the companies or industries or projects concerned. If a company cannot finance a project from its own resources, and cannot obtain backing from the big and efficient London capital market, the implication is that after a highly expert and experienced appraisal, the project has been judged unlikely to show an adequate return on the resources involved. Similarly, if companies in difficulty in a declining industry cannot obtain resources to keep them going and enable themselves to adapt to contemporary conditions, it means that their chances of successful adaptation are rated extremely low by the collective wisdom and experience of the money market. While the City's judgment can, of course, be wrong, it is unlikely to be so in more than a small proportion of the cases which eventually emerge as claimants for Government backing. Thus most of the requests from private industry for Government financial backing are either invitations to accept a poor and chancy profit on a large amount of resources, or to accept a certain loss.

Another variant on industry's approaches to the Government is the search for 'soft' capital. It is quite common for Government loans to industry to be made at considerably less than the market interest rate for comparable purposes. There is thus a substantial inducement for industrialists to approach the Government for help even when finance might conceivably be raised through normal channels. In some cases the Government finds itself enabling companies to make higher profits by thus subsidising interest charges. In other cases it effectively gives the go-ahead for projects which are only viable at a subsidised interest rate and would not have been undertaken at normal interest charges. What all this amounts to is diversion of resources by the Government into projects which on straight economic terms would not go ahead, but would instead be replaced by other projects with a higher prospective profitability.

The theory which underlies this kind of diversion of resources has two prongs. The first is that there may be some projects which, while not sufficiently profitable to be undertaken as ordinary commercial ventures, are nevertheless of sufficient economic benefit to the nation to justify Government sponsorship. This is a highly debatable proposition, usually supported by arguments about import saving or the use of resources which already exist, or providing some kind of base from which other independently viable developments can stem. Saving imports by subsidised or protected uneconomic home manufacture is rarely of long term benefit to an economy, since it means that domestic users have to pay an enhanced price, directly or indirectly, for their requirements. If existing resources cannot be used without some kind of subsidy it again means that they are not economic by world standards and that domestic users of their products are penalised. The idea of Government 'pump-priming' to get some new or developing industry going has more superficial attractions, though it rarely works out as well in practice as theory predicts. Britain's extremely costly pioneering in atomic energy, for example, has shown an extremely poor payoff as measured in terms of international competitiveness.

One of the essential weaknesses of the case for Government subsidies for either declining or growing industries is the sheer difficulty of making a sensible choice among all the candidates, all of whom, as we have seen, are likely to have been turned down as normal commercial propositions. The idea that there is some collective wisdom available to politicians and civil servants which enables them to choose winners from among projects which have been turned down by bankers and the stock markets seems decidedly whimsical. What is, in fact, likely to happen is that projects will be selected either on the basis of the amount of pressure which their proponents can mount, or because they fire the imagination or political sensitivities of a particular Minister.

An equally damaging factor with State backed projects is their tendency to use funds with an extravagance and lack of control which would not be found in the normal commercial enterprise. The all-too familiar pattern with the Government financed project is an eventual cost enormously in excess of the original estimates— Concorde and the cancelled TSR-2 are obvious examples. There are various reasons for such escalation, but it is difficult to avoid the conclusion that obscuring or abandoning the profit motive through Government backing strongly predisposes to extravagance.

A NON-INTERVENTIONIST FUTURE?

It would be exaggeratedly dogmatic to conclude from this survey that governments should never intervene in industry. Our study does, however, go beyond suggesting that much of what the Labour Government attempted between 1964 and 1968 was doomed to be self-defeating because it was too grandiose, too doctrinaire, too bureaucratic, and left too much industrial decision making to politicians and others who were simply not competent to undertake it. What it also appears to indicate—and this may well be our most important conclusion—is that State intervention in industry is a much less powerful instrument than its advocates have always supposed.

It can very easily do harm to the economy, but to achieve really major beneficial changes requires intervention on a scale which would be unacceptable in a society with any pretensions to being non-authoritarian. Bringing about major changes by Government incentive or subsidy implies a diversion of resources so great that the economic distortions would probably be insupportable. Bringing about major changes by Government prescription and control implies an apparatus of detailed direction which would closely approximate to totalitarianism.

If this analysis is correct, it has a clear and important bearing on the policies which future British Governments, irrespective of their political persuasions, should adopt. It should mean, in effect, an end to the search for economic panaceas which has constituted such a blind alley for Britain, under both Conservative and Labour administrations during the 1960s. It should mean the end of political campaigns promising 'instant' improvement in our national fortunes as politicians apply their omniscient touch to the improvement of industrial efficiency. Above all, it should mean the end of our nominally free society reaching for interventionist, authoritarian solutions as soon as it runs into problems. The implication would obviously be the recognition that a free enterprise society requires free enterprise solutions to problems.

It is no part of the function of this book to suggest that some 'instant' right wing solution exists for Britain's admitted economic problems. The economy will only be restored to health by the return of British industry to world standards of dedication, efficiency and competitiveness. This is bound to be a process whose completion will be measured in terms of a decade or so rather than in the early years of a single government.

It is not difficult, however, to suggest the broad lines on which such a restorative process should proceed. The first essential is a period of stability. It may well be necessary that such stability should take place at a relatively low level of prosperity, but a guaranteed period of sound money, free from arbitrary and unpredictable change, would at least restore to British industry the possibility of planning ahead with reasonable confidence. While such a period would nominally have as its prime intention, the maintenance of some kind of *status quo*, its end-product might well be a surge of economic growth such as Britain has not experienced among the feverish (and mostly retrograde) changes of the 1960s.

During this period of relative quiet our Government could carry out studies of a subject which has received all too little attention in recent years while the vogue for intervention has held sway: the studies should try to determine the circumstances in which the free enterprise industrial society can make most rapid progress.

It would not be surprising if such research showed that industry in the market economy makes most rapid progress when it is given maximum incentive and maximum pressure of competition. Such principles have often been suggested in recent years, but only in Western Germany and the United States have they been put into practice in any comprehensive way. It may well be that after years of regulation, frustration, quasi-monopoly, and persistent attacks on the profit motive, British industry would require larger incentives to stimulate rapid advances than are given in the successful nations with whom we try to compete. Provision of substantial incentives to corporate success and individual effort would doubtless run counter to many ingrained prejudices, but is there any real objection to allowing some of our citizens to get rich, or to allow money to fructify in company coffers, if the British nation achieved a major advance in prosperity in the process?

Adoption of such a philosophy would clearly reduce the scope for politicians who feel compelled to justify their existence or theories by continual intervention in the economy. There would still remain plenty for them to do, however. The function of the politician would be—and surely should be—to create the environment in which industry could best thrive. Among the requirements would be the creation of an infra-structure far in advance of anything which Britain has yet contemplated, and assistance in the provision of facilities and conditions in which the nation could enjoy prosperity and leisure well beyond what even the most persuasive political spokesmen have so far promised.

There would even be scope for some residual political intervention in industry. Doubtless industrialists could agree among themselves on a variety of modest and practical schemes in which they would like the Government's help. An economy in which free enterprise industry was genuinely forging ahead would also be rich enough to afford the occasional state-sponsored spectacular technological project which might give, with luck, a major stake in future world developments.

State intervention has failed in both of Britain's major political parties. While the forms of intervention adopted by the Labour Government have often been such as to ensure their own failure, we have suggested that all the evidence implies that attempts to transform the economy through State intervention would in any case have been unsuccessful unless the process were carried to the point of turning Britain into an authoriatrian state. What has not been attempted, in any whole-hearted way, is to speed economic progress by liberating and fostering the dynamism and creativity currently lying dormant in British industry.

This, surely, is the way forward.

INDEX

Index